Raise Your Visibility On LinkedIn

Louise Brogan

RaisePress Publishing.

Editor: Lynn Brown lynn@lynn-brown.co.uk

Design: Scott Thompson scott@rorschach.co.uk

First edition 2024.

Contents

Acknowledgements

This book has been a long time coming. I have wanted to write a book since I was about age seven and at primary school. I always thought it would be a fictional book. So thank you to my P4 teacher, Mrs Mills, who inspired a lifelong love of reading and writing.

My dad always said you can be whatever you want to be, you just need to do the work. So here I am, dad, an author. Wish you were here to see it.

Thanks to my dream book team of Lynn Brown for editing, Scott Thompson for typesetting, Jill Pryor for cover design, Tiffanie Smith for helping with the darn publishing, and Heather Sills for proofreading.

Thanks to my own team of Nicola Rattle, Tara Torrens, Amanda Sloan, Vikkie Richmond, Holly Molloy, Nicholas Simon and Tiffanie Smith for being amazing and helping me build this business I love.

Thanks to Alison Jones of Practical Inspiration Publishing for taking my Sunday morning writings and helping me to create a Table of Contents that I could actually work with.

Huge thanks to the people who allowed me to feature their stories: Fiona Walsh, Mary O'Driscoll, Ann Handley, Professor Kerensa Jennings, Sarah Reveiilard, Oliver Banks, Nigel Cliffe, Sarah Burgess and Jenny Stilwell.

Thanks Sarah Russo, Charlotte Hughes Huntley, Melina Palmer, Shelli Warren, Elizabeth Cook, Oliver Banks, Lucy Eckley, Tom Martin, Luke Sherran, Alex Curtis, Sarah Robinson, Miranda von Fricken, Janine Coombes, Natalie Eckdahl and Amy Woods, who all either gave input, cheered me on, or simply inspired me.

I wrote this book on Sunday mornings before the rest of the house was up and out of bed. So the biggest thanks go to my family, for giving me the time and space to write. Thank you to Diarmuid, Sarah, Daithi and Shay and to my mum, sisters and brother, who are my biggest cheerleaders.

Are you using LinkedIn?

LinkedIn has become the go-to social media platform for a lot of people, especially since the Covid-19 pandemic. In 2024, there are more than 1 billion LinkedIn accounts – pre-pandemic numbers sat at around 700 million.[1] LinkedIn has adapted for this new audience, adding in features like video and newsletters.

The idea behind this book is to help real people use LinkedIn.[2] Who do I mean by 'real people'? People who run small businesses. People who work in corporate firms. Podcasters. Coaches. Consultants. Marketing managers.

People who want to build a network, get business (or a promotion) from networking on the platform, and who want to understand what to do when they are logged in. People like you.

How to use LinkedIn when you are in business: the core steps

This is not a book on how to become a Top Voice, or get 40 leads a month, or grow a following of half a million (even though I have met some of these people and it turns out they are also real people).

The goal of this book is that you feel a bit more comfortable using LinkedIn, a bit braver and a bit more informed as to how to go about it.

Throughout the book, I'll share some stories of real people using LinkedIn for purposes from getting on podcasts to becoming a member of the board of directors, and all the things in between.

So, let's dive in ...

---

[1] *'LinkedIn business highlights from Microsoft's FY20 Q4 earnings', 23 July 2020. Available at: https://news.linkedin.com/2020/july/linkedin-business-highlights-from-microsoft-s-fy20-q4-earnings*

[2] *'Not real' people include those who are using automation to spam you, accounts using third-party software tools or AI to create their content, or simply people who work in sales and have to use LinkedIn in a very specific lead-generation style. While I have no issues with salespeople, this book is aimed at the rest of you.*

I started my own business from need rather than choice. From selling Avon to my mum's church friends as a teenager, to hosting full-scale formal dinner dances at university, my entrepreneurial streak was always a project somewhere in the background.

Once I qualified with my MSc in Computing and Information Systems at 25 years old, I put all that aside. (Yes, I took a gap year backpacking in between, to find myself.) I became a software engineer. Then an IT project manager. For almost 11 years. When I became a mum, my career hit the brakes a little bit. I started to work part-time to juggle motherhood with three small children and my ambitions.

I wanted to go further in my role at work but was 'guided' into believing that I would not get another level up in my role unless I went back full-time, which was not for me. I started to think about what I could do, and the social media work began.

I loved working for myself, but I was cautious. Rather than throw myself off a cliff and build my parachute on the way down (do mums of three tend to be reckless? I think not), I saved as much money as I could until I could replace my salary. Then I quit.

Running a social media business in 2013 was a whole lot different to today. For starters, people only wanted help with Facebook and Twitter. I don't think I had a LinkedIn client until about 2017.

I loved that stage of business. Trying to figure everything out. Learning how to sell. What worked – connections and community – and what didn't – trying to build an email list and launch an online course at $99 did not fulfil my internet dreams.

Starting to grow

A few things turned the corner for me …

Travelling

I remember the first time I flew to London to engage with business networks outside of my local Northern Ireland area. Terrifying! But taking a step forward really paid off. I joined UK-based masterminds and attended conferences in London. I surrounded myself both in person and online with like-minded people.

Coaching

Around the same time, I started working with a coach. I have never regretted investing in outside support to help my business. Well, one or two of those investments didn't quite work out the way I was promised, but I ended up learning a few lessons all the same. When you are looking for a coach, follow them for a while online, and listen to them on a podcast or watch them in a video interview. See if someone you trust can recommend a coach for you.

Niching down

My long-term coach, Natalie Eckdahl, recommended I 'niche down' to a particular social media platform. I thought long and hard about this. (Thanks Natalie!) I chose LinkedIn because when I spent time there, I earned business much more quickly than I did on Facebook or Instagram. Plus, those clients had more money to spend. Plus, no one else seemed to want to specialise in LinkedIn. It paid off for me – especially when the pandemic arrived. More on that later …

Creating content

I launched a podcast – initially about women who were starting a small business – called the Social Bee Podcast. I hosted local events and built my network. And I pivoted. Several times.

The podcast turned into a LinkedIn-focused podcast. The network expanded across the UK, Ireland, USA/Canada, and Australia and New Zealand.

I kept showing up.

A note about resilience

When I was young, I was part of a swimming club. We trained five times a week. I was a good swimmer but never a brilliant one. I remember my dad saying to me, 'Louise, you are so good at long distance.' Put me in a pool and I will just keep going. I didn't win any sprints and rarely made a final at a swimming gala. I did once swim 5 km for charity though, with no breaks (that's 200 lengths for any non-swimmers reading).

Maybe it's stubbornness – a common trait found in people from Belfast. Maybe it's resilience built up from being one of four children. Whatever it is, I used it in my business.

When it comes to content marketing, I approach it like a tortoise, not a hare. And I change direction when I need to.

My original Social Bee Podcast was fun to create, but it didn't lead to any particular business. When I began switching to create episodes about how to use LinkedIn, I found a bigger audience. I also started to get invited onto other people's podcasts to talk about LinkedIn from an expert's point of view.

I wrote about LinkedIn. I created videos about LinkedIn. I made podcasts about LinkedIn. I started to be referred to people who were looking for help with their LinkedIn.

When you niche down and share content that helps people with the area you are an expert in, you become very referable.

Meeting the King

Then I met the King.

In 2017, I applied to be in the Small Business Saturday top 100 businesses in the UK, and was successful. I found my people in this group of small business supporters. (The definition of a small business in the UK is one that has fewer than 250 employees.) In the Small Business Saturday group, I met fellow 'microbusiness' owners. (A microbusiness is generally defined as having fewer than 10 employees or less than £250,000 in annual revenue.) We had similar issues and struggles, and could really relate to one another – as well as support each other.

Since 2018 I have been a Small Business Champion in the UK. I have hosted events, netwalks and webinars, and offered free advice to this group of entrepreneurs.

In 2022, though, I got something I did not expect. Or believe. An invitation to Buckingham Palace for a small business reception arrived by email. I still don't know how my name was added to the list, but I know that raising my visibility and showing up online had something to do with it.

When the email arrived, I didn't believe it was real. I went to LinkedIn. I looked up the emailer to see if they were genuine. Someone in my network was connected to the emailer, so I sent off a private message on LinkedIn to ask if they knew this person. And they did!

Not only did I end up being invited to Buckingham Palace, along with 400 other representatives from the small business community in the UK, but I also learned I was on 'The List'. Ten of us had been selected to meet the King ahead of the larger group, including Anne Boden, founder of Starling Bank, and Peter Jones from *Dragons' Den*. It remains the highlight event of my career, though I have no idea what I said to King Charles. The official invitation sits in a frame on the wall behind my desk, along with my photos of me meeting the King.

Raising your visibility on LinkedIn

This book focuses specifically on LinkedIn, but you can apply a lot of it to other platforms and media too. Choose your medium. Pick a niche. Show up. Talk about it, share your knowledge with others, and build connection and community. My efforts on LinkedIn have led to countless podcast appearances and invites, as well as being the main source of leads for our business. I hope this book helps you to create the same.

Chapter **1**

Your current view of LinkedIn

In this chapter:

What do you think of LinkedIn?

Be honest.

You might have thought that LinkedIn is the place where people go when they need a new job. Maybe you created a profile years ago, and only visit LinkedIn when your boss asks you to comment on a Company Page post.

If you are like my mum, you might have heard of LinkedIn, but you stick to Facebook.

You went to a conference once where someone spoke about how to grow your business using Instagram, and you tried creating reels for a month before sinking into exhaustion and going back to good old-fashioned word of mouth.

If you are over 40, like me, then you entered the world of work when all you had to worry about was getting the right information on your three-page CV/résumé. That was tough enough! Now it's all digital.

A typical comment or question I get on my YouTube channel, which is all about LinkedIn, goes something like this: 'I'm locked out of my LinkedIn account. I need it because I am switching jobs. HELP!'

This person probably only ever looks at their LinkedIn when they are ready to move jobs. But LinkedIn is not just for jobseekers.

Why aren't you posting on LinkedIn?

In my experience, a lot of people are resistant to using LinkedIn to its fullest effect for a variety of reasons.

Quite simply, they aren't sure what to say. It is easier to follow people and scroll through the newsfeed than it is to come up with something interesting to write about.

The main content creators on LinkedIn tend to be entrepreneurs and business owners who recognise the need to grow their personal brand. Content creators make up a very small percentage of the people who are on LinkedIn. Depending on which research you read, estimates vary from 3% to 10% of users posting on LinkedIn in any given month.[3]

[3] *Three million users post on LinkedIn every week, in an audience of 1 billion users. Source: '100+ LinkedIn statistics you need to know in 2024', 11 September 2024, SocialPilot. Available at: https://socialpilot.co/blog/linkedin-statistics*

Lyndsay Cambridge is a business owner who was not really embracing LinkedIn, despite working with other business owners. We worked together on her profile and she discovered a different perspective on how to use LinkedIn:

Louise is just a genius when it comes to LinkedIn. It had never occurred to me that with the right LinkedIn strategy I would get clients directly from the platform!

By following Louise's advice I've gone from hating LinkedIn to it being my favourite platform – one that delivers leads and sales. LinkedIn is now my favourite place to be.

If you have a network of 200 connections, and only three of those people are 'creators', then you might think that posting on LinkedIn annoys your network, or that you are posting too often. However, imagine if over time you built up that network to 2,000 people. And then you posted twice a week. But don't overthink it. You won't spam your network if you follow the guidance in this book.

How the LinkedIn newsfeed works

Think about it:

- LinkedIn personalises the newsfeed to each user
- LinkedIn wants to keep people on the platform for as long as possible.

The way the company makes money is through advertising (and its Premium services, of course). If you spend 20 minutes scrolling on LinkedIn, you will probably see a couple of adverts. In fact, there are a lot more adverts on your screen than you realise, but as they are usually quite discreet you can focus on your network and your newsfeed and ignore them.

When you post something on LinkedIn, only a small percentage of your network sees your post. If you start to get comments on that post, the algorithm picks this up and shows your post to more of your network.

Tagging

If you tag people in a post, LinkedIn may restrict who it shows the post to in terms of a mutual network of the people you have tagged.

What does this mean?

If I write a post and tag Lyndsay in it, the post will be shared with mutual connections of ours but possibly not a wider audience. If I write about Lyndsay and don't tag her, this changes who the post will be shown to.

'But that's not fair!' I hear you cry.

Maybe not, but it's how the platform works. We need to figure out how we can use it to our best advantage.

Top **Tip** **Tag with caution!**

Throughout this book, I will share some stories from clients and friends on why they are using LinkedIn. Here's the first …

Case Study **Jenny Stilwell, strategy advisor, business mentor, author**

When I first joined Louise's *LinkedIn Mastermind*,[4] it was because I needed a new strategy on how to use LinkedIn to build my network and influence reach. I was completing the manuscript for my second book, and LinkedIn was a part of my marketing strategy.

We had a great group in Louise's Mastermind – all service professionals with plenty of experience and credentials, but needing help in terms of how to harness LinkedIn as a marketing tool. Louise is not only the LinkedIn expert, she is also hilarious and great fun to work with.

My strategy has been 'narrow and deep', not 'wide and generic', so my network is small, but it has been amazing. I have connections from around the world – especially Australia (where I'm based), New Zealand and the UK. This focus has been deliberate. I love my network! I've been able to collaborate with my LinkedIn peers on a strategic retreat, and secure some fabulous people to be guest speakers at retreats and act as podcast guests. I honestly have great relationships with people I feel I've known forever, but I haven't met all of them in person (yet). We can send each other messages requesting feedback on projects and new ideas, and it's great to have access to input from people whose opinions you value.

When I launched my book, *The 7% Club: How To Be One of the 7% of Businesses That Make It Beyond $2m in Turnover*, I of course used LinkedIn. The book has sold all around the world, and I've been approached by all sorts of people to be a guest for their podcast or event as a result, and it has opened all sorts of conversations.

My approach and focus with LinkedIn have completely changed since Louise's Mastermind. I don't bother with any other social media channel because LinkedIn is where my clients, collaborators and peers are.

[4] *LinkedIn Mastermind is a monthly online small-group session for like-minded entrepreneurs and business owners who want to build their presence on LinkedIn. Find out more here: https://louisebrogan.com/everything-you-need-to-know-when-you-invest-in-my-6-month-linkedin-mastermind/*

Chapter **2**

How to approach LinkedIn as a 'networking event'

In this chapter:

The LinkedIn analogy

Consider LinkedIn as the online version of your favourite in-person industry event. Somewhere you go to listen to great speakers, find like-minded professionals, swap business details and even set up follow-up meetings with potential clients.

Sounds great! But how do you do that?

Here are some of the things we'll work through in the upcoming chapters …

- **Prepare for the event:** We are going to look at how to optimise your profile or dress yourself for heading to a professional event.
- **Check out in advance who is speaking:** Start to follow interesting people and thought leaders on the platform.
- **Be intentional:** If you are going to spend time on this platform, set yourself goals on how many people you want to connect with and how many posts you plan to share in a week. You should also set a goal for how many posts you will leave comments on.

Arriving at the event

When you go to an in-person event, how do you behave?

It might look something like this: you walk through the door and register; someone gives you a name badge; you look around to see if there is anyone you know.

If you do see someone you know, say hello. If you don't, one tip I always find useful is to walk up to a group of three or more people. The form this takes on LinkedIn is starting to comment on a post where others are also commenting.

During the event

Logging into LinkedIn, scrolling and leaving again without commenting or connecting with anyone is the equivalent of heading to a conference, walking in to hear the speakers, getting your coffee and leaving without ever speaking to anyone.

You might have benefited from listening to a talk, but you could have made so much more of the whole experience by starting a conversation with the person standing/sitting beside you who is listening to the same speaker.

This is the real-life equivalent of connecting with the other people in the comments on the post you just read.

My goal for you, of course, is that over time you will become the person who is speaking on the stage. The person creating the posts! And the network will be turning up to read/hear what you have to say and having conversations about it. Sounds good, right?

LinkedIn vs other social media

If we compare LinkedIn to other social media platforms, what makes it different?

First, it is recognised for the professional behaviour of its members. Companies that may not allow their employees to spend time on Instagram, TikTok or Pinterest during the working day actively encourage them to take to LinkedIn.

When someone goes to LinkedIn, they are already thinking about their business network. TikTok and Instagram are viewed as more for fun, and Facebook is for friends and family.

What about Twitter? When Twitter was purchased by Elon Musk and renamed X, many people decided to leave the platform and a lot of them headed over to LinkedIn.

Some LinkedIn experts say that this is why LinkedIn introduced the concept of 'followers' as well as connections – to appease the Twitterati. However, LinkedIn lacks the negativity that can be found on X and – although we do have conversations in our newsfeeds – unlike X, I recommend that you don't post on LinkedIn more than once a day. If you are someone who likes to give a running commentary on events, LinkedIn is not the place to do it.

One group of professionals that remains resistant to LinkedIn's charms is journalists. They prefer to poke fun at LinkedIn, and portray it as stuffy, or suggest that updates are 'cringe'.[5] This is a shame, as a lot of interesting discussions are happening on LinkedIn.

LinkedIn is also after the news market. It makes no secret of it. As with Facebook, there is a race to become the place where most people get their daily news, and they both want to be the winner.[6]

[5] *'Elon Musk is helping make LinkedIn cringe more attractive', Business Insider, 3 January 2024. Available at: https://businessinsider.com/linkedin-cringe-more-attractive-advertisers-than-elon-musk-x-2024-1*

[6] *Social media and news fact sheet, Pew Research Center, 17 September 2024. Available at: https://pewresearch.org/journalism/fact-sheet/social-media-and-news-fact-sheet/*

Chapter **3**

Why you and your team should be using LinkedIn

In this chapter:

There are more than one billion registered accounts on LinkedIn. It is widely recognised as the main B2B social media platform.[7] If you want to build your business and brand online, you need to be on LinkedIn.

It is a trusted online resource, which is one of its unique selling points. LinkedIn has been recognised as one of the most trusted social media sites for five consecutive years according to *Insider Intelligence's US Digital Trust Benchmark (2022)*.[8] My theory here is that because most people's employers are also on the platform, they tend to behave themselves! That doesn't mean you can't meet some trolls or undesirables there.

When I was a teenager, I participated in the Duke of Edinburgh's Award (DofE).[9] My old DofE leader used to say to us, when we were heading out into the Mourne Mountains armed only with our camping stoves and tents, 'Watch out for undesirables.' I never actually met any of these undesirables, only some sheep and a few random farmers.

Luckily for me, it's been the same on LinkedIn. Not the sheep and the farmers but, in general, very few undesirables gracing my newsfeed or network.

As with DofE expeditions, this takes a little planning. And strategy. If you take care about who you let into your network, then your experience is going to be a little easier.

Although we take a brief look at this next, in Chapter 5 we'll look in detail at how to build your network in a way that adds value for you.

Your network

My goal is for you to build a network of value on LinkedIn, but what does that mean?

Imagine having your LinkedIn network full of people you want to be connected to.

People who are interesting. They share ideas and articles that you find value in. They don't need to have huge followings. For example, because I am really interested in finding out more about growing my YouTube channel, I follow YouTube experts who share useful tips. I am not interested in some marketing bro blowing hot air about their millions of views.

---

[7] B2B stands for 'business to business', i.e. where businesses work with other businesses; as opposed to B2C, which stands for 'business to consumer'.

[8] 'Digital Trust Benchmark 2022: social platforms lose ground as user trust falls', 16 September 2022. Available at: https://insiderintelligence.com/content/digital-trust-benchmark-2022

Everyone is different, though. And every person's network on LinkedIn is unique to them.

The key is to enjoy spending time there, which is much more likely when you are a bit more selective about who you connect with or follow.

You will also want to connect with people who are interested in what you have to say. The people who subscribe to your newsletter. Who follow your content – and sometimes even comment on it.

When you share a post on LinkedIn, isn't it great when people start to leave genuine, real comments on it? That only happens when you make real connections with your network.

It goes both ways, of course. If you never comment on anyone else's content, then why would they comment on yours?

I see a lot of LinkedIn Top Voices who share something with their network, and then don't respond to a single comment. This is the opposite of what I want for you on LinkedIn.

In my opinion, it is much better to have a small network who regularly have back-and-forth conversations in comments on your posts. Back at our in-person conference, this is the equivalent of sitting at exactly the right networking table. The one you enjoy being at. Not the rowdy one next door. The one for *you*.

Case **Study** | **Nigel Cliffe, LinkedIn consultant**

Nigel Cliffe, a Yorkshire-based LinkedIn consultant, shares his thoughts on what size of audience to build …

It depends on your goal and what your strategy is.

If you are aiming to be an influencer of some sort, seeking speaking gigs, for example, as an outcome, then mass audiences might suit you.

For most of us, developing trust in our personal brand step by step is what it's all about – well it is for me, anyway.

I think it's only polite to reply to people who have kindly commented on my posts. For this reason, I don't publish posts as frequently as many, because I'd rather maximise the value of the live post than start another one.

[9] *The Duke of Edinburgh's Award is a fabulous thing that young people in the UK can do, involving volunteering, skills, and the infamous camping and hiking expeditions into the wilds, depending on where you live and how closely your DofE leaders stick to the vision of the original Duke of Edinburgh, Prince Philip.*

Choosing other people to have in our network is a bit more strategic. Think about the people who have the connections and contacts you need for your next stage of growth.

Let's say you work with women who want to find podcast guests. They could connect with other podcasters who serve a similar audience. In the comments of those other podcaster posts is where you can find your potential guests.

It is much better to build a small and mighty network of relevant people on LinkedIn than to accept anyone and everyone who reaches out to you.

LinkedIn has set limits on how many people you can connect with in any given month. Most users are limited to connecting with 100 people per week. This makes sense to me – if you want to connect with people authentically and exchange messages, it would be hard to do this with more than 100 people.

> **Top Tip**
>
> In 2024, we can be 'followed' by people without having to connect with them. Just because someone sends you a connection request doesn't mean you have to accept it.
>
> Don't worry about offending someone by ignoring their connection request – we are in the professional world here (unless it's your next-door neighbour's husband and you know you are having dinner with them on Saturday night; maybe don't ignore that one – you can unfollow him on Monday).

Your profile

Start by updating the key areas of your profile. If someone is going to do you a favour and introduce you to a key person of interest, make sure that when they visit your profile, it looks smart and relevant.

Key areas to tackle are your headline, your About summary and your Experience section. For more on this, see Chapter 12.

You can update the rest of your profile in time, but those three areas will be key for now.

> **Top Tip**
>
> Get an up-to-date headshot on your profile. Don't show up for your next interview or sales call and surprise the person on the other end as you have suddenly aged 10 years. Embrace your wrinkles!

Engaging with your network

Now that you are starting to get the right people into your network, and your profile is up to date, we can dip a toe in the water of using LinkedIn by commenting on other people's posts.

This is easier to do with people you have just connected with. It's even better if you have met them in person at a recent event.

One way to do this, without feeling awkward, can be to engage on posts from thought leaders in your industry. They are used to people they don't know commenting on their posts.

> **Top Tip**
>
> You may not have noticed this, but Company Page posts get very few comments, so it is easy to stand out by commenting on one: maybe your own Company Page, or the Company Page of a target client.
>
> Read the post and think of something relevant to say. Don't just write 'Thanks' or 'Good idea'. Consider what you might say if you met someone from this organisation at their booth at a conference and go from there. Ask a question!

Writing a post

You will find that as you course-correct your network and begin commenting on posts, you should start to get some more people visiting your profile. Ideally, this will give you the confidence boost you need to write your own posts.

Another easy win here is to share the last post from your Company Page, and write about *why* and *what* you found interesting in that post that your audience may be interested in.

If you don't have a Company Page, then think about what your ideal client or connection would be interested in. Share an article from a journal or newspaper that relates to your industry.

Be aware that when you share a post with a link, you may not get as much reach. However, when it suits the post I want to share, I go ahead and include the link. One way to deal with this restriction is to add your link in the first comment of your post. This only works if you are posting in real time. If you want to schedule your content, go ahead and put the link in your post.

> **Top Tip**
>
> LinkedIn News shares 10 stories each day that it believes are relevant to you based on either your industry or your location. If you see an article you can comment on, go ahead – and then share it with your own network and give your take on this article.
>
> I have worked with several clients who have taken this advice and have been featured by the LinkedIn News team as a result. Of course, bear in mind my earlier advice – if you only write 'Great news!', no one is going to feature you. Write something relevant and spark conversation.

This stuff takes time – you won't do all these things overnight. But even by getting this far in this book, I think you are going to take at least the first step. Hey, you could even share a line from the book with your audience and say why you think they might like it.

Very meta.

Chapter **4**

How to get over your fear of posting on LinkedIn

In this chapter:

Getting started

In February 2024, I spoke to a conference room of more than 65 women about using LinkedIn to help raise the profile of their businesses. We had a Q&A session at the end and one very familiar question came up from the audience: 'How do you get over the fear of posting?'

Having spoken to and trained thousands of people on how to use LinkedIn, I hear this all the time.

Many of my clients have come from working in a corporate role. Maybe they decided to launch a business to fit around their family life. Maybe they got to the age of 50 and decided to retrain as a coach or launch their consultancy business to get more from work.

The main *fear* comes from overthinking what your peers will think.

- Who are you to write about your industry on LinkedIn?
- What will your colleagues think when they read what you wrote in your last post?
- Maybe your whole network is full of people you have met through your career, and you are literally too frozen from fear of what they might think to post anything. Never mind if one of them replies to your post!

I have a strategy to help. Meet Jane …

Jane worked in a high-paced HR role. Having experienced stress at work due to trying to juggle looking after small children with travelling into London for work and keeping herself sane, she decided she wanted to try self-employment.

When Jane came to me, she had been setting up her business for about six months, had a website, had completed her coaching certificates and had been getting work through word of mouth. She knew her business would work if she could get a steadier stream of referrals.

LinkedIn seemed to be the place to network and win business. But she was starting to feel those old feelings again, of stress and anxiety …

What if she started writing posts on LinkedIn and her ex-colleagues were reading them? What on earth would she write about? She wasn't an expert. People in her old London network knew far more about this stuff than she did …

That is OK!

No one is expecting you to write posts on LinkedIn as the premier thought leader in your space. Rather than broadcasting at people in your newsfeed, try starting a conversation with them.

When you reset how you see LinkedIn, this becomes so much easier.

After working with Jane for six months, she became comfortable showing up on LinkedIn, writing posts and starting a newsletter. Our next step was to start creating short-form marketing videos to showcase her thought leadership – one of my favourite ways to work with clients.

We now create content for Jane every month using our LinkedIn video marketing service.[10] She shows up to our call once a month, and I record video content with her, which we are then able to chop up and use to create multiple posts.

Not only does this make Jane's life easier, but she now has a bank of video content to use in future on other platforms as well as LinkedIn.

[10] *Find out more here: https://louisebrogan.com/linkedin-marketing/*

Let's hear from another of my clients – Mary O'Driscoll of Cork, Ireland.

Mary had left her pharma role to start her own business. This was her experience with LinkedIn …

Case Study | **Mary O'Driscoll, strategic consultant, Cork, Ireland**

In February 2023, I launched my life science supply chain consulting business on LinkedIn, thinking, 'Here I am, I am great and I'll be beating people away from my door I'll have so much work.'

And, yes, I did get work from LinkedIn – an amazing achievement as my account was so bad.

Falling into the classic trap of all supply chain professionals – i.e. thinking that marketing is not a real job – I was flapping around for six months before realising I had, arrogantly, underestimated the need and complexity of marketing.

Having spent another two months bouncing around 'marketing experts' trying to convince me that Instagram was my key platform, I finally had the cop-on to ask for a recommendation for an actual LinkedIn marketing expert, aka Louise Brogan!

It would be a waste of time to say what I thought marketing and LinkedIn were, as I was so totally clueless. The best analogy is, I was a baby learning how to roll!

Eight months later, I am now able to walk confidently – albeit slowly – on LinkedIn.

How has my opinion changed over those eight months, and how has Louise driven those changes?

Now I understand and can apply:

- the global power and reach of LinkedIn
- how LinkedIn can be used effectively to ground and provide credibility for you and your company
- the relevant mechanics of LinkedIn
- how LinkedIn, content marketing, lead generation, networking and sales connect together.

How LinkedIn ties everything together:

- people buy from people and not from companies
- how to leverage LinkedIn by posting photos and relevant personal information (my next big step is video!)
- how LinkedIn can be used to market effectively high-value niche service offerings.

For content marketing:

- short, relevant posts are better than long, boring ones
- a certain level of repetition is OK
- the power of the algorithm
- keywords
- always have a call to action.

And finally, LinkedIn can be interesting and useful.

If, like Jane and Mary, you think I could support you too – not just with LinkedIn but with your business goals too, please take a look at the Resources section at the end of the book to find out more.

LinkedIn: a positive social media platform

The good news is that the LinkedIn network is a relatively positive crowd. My most engaged posts ever have been where I have shared big wins in my business – my network was so happy for me and celebrated alongside me.

Why is this?

Most people on LinkedIn are connected to their colleagues, so they behave more professionally. No hiding behind @ handles that don't reflect your actual name. It is my belief that most people are decent. If they aren't, then the easy answer is to remove them from your network and, if necessary, block them.

Bear these positive people in mind when you create a post. Start by grabbing a sheet of paper and writing down all the things people ask you about your services/ products. Here's an example ...

Example 1: How to come up with LinkedIn posts

What are the FAQs you get from your business network? Start keeping a note of them.

Here are some of the commonly asked questions I get about using LinkedIn:

- What do I say?
- Do I need Premium?
- What software do you use for video?
- My network is full of people from my old job – is that OK?
- I'm doing two things – how can I market my business while still working in my career?

Once you have a list of several such questions, you can start writing down some ideas about posts to create. Take one of these key FAQs and expand on it.

Let's take a question about video: 'How do you create video for LinkedIn?' Immediately, I can come up with four posts I can write:

- What tech/software/editing tools do I need?
- What to say on video and how long should it be?
- How can I repurpose these videos?
- How do I add captions to my video?

Start with a written post. Add images or video. You can talk about the same thing multiple times.

Do you need to be an expert?

Definition of an expert: a person who has special skill or knowledge in some field; specialist; authority; a language expert.

Are you an expert? Who are you to give an opinion? Why would anyone want to hear what you have to say?

During conversations I have had with many individuals (usually during training sessions), the discussion can veer around to showing up as an expert. You may feel that you are a bit of a fraud, and you don't see yourself as the expert in your field. That's OK. Let's dive into this a bit more …

I believe you can join a conversation about something on LinkedIn without being an expert in it, and I want to explain why you should.

We don't all need to be experts

Let's leave LinkedIn and play with a little imagination here.

If you can remove yourself from the entire situation for a moment, imagine you are at a neighbourhood BBQ or you have taken your dog out for a walk, and while at the dog park/beach/local community centre, you come across a few other people.

They are discussing the new community garden that has sprung up in your area.

You walk past this green space a few times a week with your dog. You have met these people in passing before (anyone with a dog will recognise this scenario – you recognise the dog but have no idea what the owner's name is) and you nod hello.

They seem to be quite animated about something. Maybe it is the garden, maybe it is the state of the pavement (sidewalk). Who are you to join in?!

- You are a member of the neighbourhood.
- You are a dog walker who uses this area.
- You are a person with independent thought!

All it takes is someone in that little cluster of neighbours to ask you what you think, and you are off to the races (not the dog races … this isn't literal remember?).

It turns out you do have some thoughts on this community garden. At the very least, you have some questions about it. So, you start to speak.

OK – so let's go back to LinkedIn.

In the community garden analogy, the community garden is the topic being discussed on LinkedIn. You are the dog walker in your personal profile.

As you are scrolling on LinkedIn, you see some of your network have 'stopped' scrolling and are having a discussion (your neighbours at the BBQ or local park).

You read the initial post (listen in to what they are saying).

You are not an expert. However, you live here and you care about the neighbourhood (you are a LinkedIn member, and you want to start building relationships on the platform and start contributing).

You read some of the comments below (your neighbours chatting about the garden – some are getting a bit hot under the collar; others are trying to send people to their shop to buy welly boots).

In the post, the original author has asked a question.

Scroll or comment? Time to be brave …

You have a choice.

You can scroll on past. Or you can stop and comment.

Maybe you want to support something someone has said in the comments, so you click 'like' on their comment. Phew … didn't get involved, can walk on with the dog and life can go on as normal.

Only thing is, your neighbours/LinkedIn network still don't know who you are!

Be brave. You do have an opinion – it doesn't have to be controversial, but you can make a comment.

The people you want to connect with, and continue the conversation with, are probably the people who silently agree with you. They just haven't been brave enough to comment yet.

Most people who view my profile on LinkedIn, or reach out to discuss how they can use LinkedIn, never comment on any of my posts, but they see them.

Example 2: Post analytics

How many times is your post shown to someone on LinkedIn? Impressions reveal how many times your post is shown to someone in their newsfeed. Let's imagine a post that has 939 'impressions'.

Of those 939 people shown the post, LinkedIn tells us that 43 people clicked the 'reaction' button. Six people commented.

When you reply to a comment, your own comment is counted. So, if you reply to the six comments with your own comments, you end up with 12 comments.

The key here is to be seen by your LinkedIn network, and everyone who has read the post and the comments has seen the profile headline, name and photo of the person commenting.

I want you to be noticed.

You know those Profile Views you get on LinkedIn? They increase with every comment you write. That's because, when you leave a comment, the other people in the community see your name, your profile photo and your headline, alongside your comment.

When you scroll on past, or even if you click on the 'like/insightful/funny' reaction button, no one knows who you are.

If you want to raise your profile on LinkedIn – your 'community' – the first step is to comment. Start to leave comments on other people's posts. Be brave – imagine I am sitting beside you and cheering you on. We can get on to writing your own posts (and even making video) later. But, for now, your first task is to leave a comment.

Then, in a week's time, check to see if your Profile Views on LinkedIn have increased. Have fun!

What about all the spammy DMs?

Stand in a room full of professionals and ask them what their number one 'hate' is about using LinkedIn and you will get this response: the spammy DMs.

A DM is a direct message. On LinkedIn, if someone has a Premium account, they can send you an InMail. More often, though, you will get a connection request from someone you don't know, and once you accept it, you can receive this sort of message:

Hi
Hope you are doing well.
I'm a YouTube marketing specialist with five years of experience. I'm interested to show my expertise by sharing your YouTube channel on various platforms. You will get 1,000+ subscribers and 2,500+ views in seven days. It's real and guaranteed results. Total cost is $70 only. You can check more packages and pricing on our website, here's the link: [...]
Let me know if you are interested.

How should you deal with these? Short answer: ignore them! If you have already accepted the person's connection request and then they send you a generic sales message, remove them from your network.

Life is too short to be sold to all the time.

Likewise, avoid doing this yourself no matter what you've been told in other books you might have read!

But if you are in sales, how can you get a sale if you can't even get a connection, I hear you cry. Well, the reason you picked up this book is to look at doing this in another way.

By sharing interesting content and starting conversations with your network – which, by the way, will be full of people who are interested in your work, if you follow my suggestions – not only will you raise your personal brand as a leader in your field, but you will also find people connect with you to ask about your services, and – even better – people start to refer others to work with you.

Sounds much better than sending out soul-sucking bland sales messages that even you feel a bit icky about, right?

There are messages you can send to someone to spark interest in your product or service, but I recommend you lead with value first. For example, maybe you have an event coming up, or a webinar you are speaking at. I have sent many messages in the DMs inviting someone to a free class I am running online.

How to craft a non-spammy sales message

- **Person A:** Sends connection request without a note (more common as LinkedIn changes its free message limit).
- **You:** Send a message thanking them for connecting with you. Check their profile – who do you have in common with them? Can you mention this in your DM?
- **Person A:** May or may not reply. Often if they have seen me on stage or heard me on a podcast, this is when they mention it.
- **You:** Thank them for tuning in and ask if they would like to sign up for your newsletter/receive the free download you mentioned in the podcast/webinar/talk.
- **Person A:** It's over to them now …

Nine times of out ten, in the conversation above, the person has heard me, or been referred, and is more than happy to get a gift in the form of a YouTube link to training or a PDF guide to using LinkedIn. Now they are on my 'nurture' list.

As for those spammy sales suggestions that you might want to hire someone you never met for $70 to let them into your business, click 'Ignore' and move on. This is a B2B professional platform – no one is getting offended!

Chapter 5

Your LinkedIn network

In this chapter:

Let's talk about people on LinkedIn. People you want to follow. People you want to talk to. People you want to do business with. And people you want to avoid!

First rule[11] of networks on LinkedIn: *You do not have to connect with everyone and anyone.*

What makes a good network on LinkedIn?

When you are more thoughtful about who you connect with, you build a network of value. Valuable content, interesting conversations and, of course, ideally it turns into monetary value if you are here to build a business.

If you are here to build your personal brand and move up the corporate ladder, value may look like mentorship, connections who can open doors for you or make introductions. The value of your network is what you decide it is.

Before we dive into the type of people to connect with on LinkedIn, I want to share a story from a friend of mine about her network and a special opportunity that came her way …

[11] *First rule of 'LinkedIn for real people' – not an actual rule.*

Story: LinkedIn for real people

Professor Kerensa Jennings FRSA

Like a lot of people, I tend to get a bit overwhelmed with the LinkedIn spam effect. So much so, I even set up a special email address to link to my LinkedIn account that I do not use for anything else.

Maybe once or twice a month, I take a look in it to see if I have missed out on anything.

Separately, I also radically pruned the sorts of notifications I get, to try to quieten the noise. But it doesn't seem to affect the sheer volume of prospecting salespeople who bombard my LinkedIn inbox with unsolicited requests to meet me. Or people who have no connection with me at all who want me to help them. Some of whom can get quite aggressive if you are unable to do so.

Having said that, for me, the pain is worth the gain. Through LinkedIn, some very, very special things have happened for me. It has proven to be a cornucopia of connections, knowledge, inspiration and credibility. And beyond that, it has led to one of the most precious things in my life. My trusteeship at Sir John Soane's Museum.

A headhunter from Green Park, the diverse recruiters, got in touch with me about the position. As it happens, I get approached a lot by recruiters, some of whom want to place me, some of whom want me to hire their candidates. On this occasion, the headhunter sent me some information via my LinkedIn inbox, asking if the museum would be of interest. My profile matched what they were looking for – someone with a background in the arts, culture or media sector who was an experienced technology executive.

My heart leapt. Sir John Soane's Museum is a place I have loved since I was a little girl. It's a time capsule, a treasure trove, a haven of precious things. A place where Roman, Greek and Egyptian artefacts jumble up in a Regency architect's house and nestle up to Canalettos and Hogarths. Priceless works of art sharing a home with antiquities representing millennia of human progress, science, design.

I had a phone call to start with, to try to understand more about the role. I went on to apply, find myself shortlisted, interviewed and then appointed. I could hardly believe how fortunate I was that, of all the people potentially suitable for the role, I was spotted in a sea of specialists.

I have LinkedIn to thank for that, and the acumen of the headhunters. I will be forever grateful for the opportunity – the Soane continues to be the jewel of my life.

I have been there more than two years now, and have loved welcoming on board our new director, Will Gompertz, as well as seeing the incredible dedication, talent and commitment of our staff and our volunteers.

It is an immense privilege to serve alongside some of the most inspiring people I have met in my life. My fellow trustees are simply wonderful, and each and every one of our executive team is exceptional. We also have a brilliant chair in Lord James Sassoon.

So I would definitely say it's worth ensuring your LinkedIn profile is sharp, reflective of you and comprehensive enough for the algorithms to select you. I can promise you, it's worth it.

Types of people to connect with on LinkedIn

Potential clients

You do need to connect with potential clients on LinkedIn. Not just so that they can see what your business does, but also so that you can see what they are sharing. When you understand what your ideal client's big issues and problems are, you can consider how your products or service could help with those issues.

Do not pitch your product as the solution to their problem unless they directly ask – for example, they write a post to say they need a new bookkeeper and are asking for recommendations. In this case, if you are a bookkeeper, feel free to reach out and message them with your service.

If your ideal client is a company or organisation, connect with key people in that company or organisation who are active on LinkedIn.

> Top **Tip**
>
> If you want to connect with a certain type of person, such as a podcaster, connect with the ones who are active on the platform. Check how many people are in their network, and if they are commenting or posting content. It is much easier to engage with someone who is active on the platform.

Strategic connections

Your strategic connections could be potential collaborators, or they could be delivering a service to your ideal clients.

Maybe your ideal client works with accountants. See which accountants they are following and connect with the ones that are active. A lot of the time, the people you want to get in front of are not posting anything on LinkedIn, but they might be reading or commenting under others' posts. Even if they don't comment or post, they will see your name and profile on the comments you leave under the mutual connection.

I work with a lot of female CEOs, and I have found that these women tend to follow female-led organisations or business coaches who work with that community. Commenting on posts that they are reading will increase the number of right-fit clients checking out my profile.

Top Tip At the time of writing (September 2024), you can only see who has viewed your profile when you upgrade to a LinkedIn Premium account.

Another group who fall under the banner of strategic connections are the people who will refer business to you. To get known by your network, keep sharing your thought leadership and helpful tips on your industry. When they are having a conversation at their next business breakfast and someone asks about the service you offer, your name will naturally come into their head.

People who are fun/interesting

I want you to enjoy reading the newsfeed on LinkedIn. Among the articles and videos from corporations, add in some people to follow who provide interesting and thought-provoking content. It is easier to comment on posts that interest you.

A lot of people who use LinkedIn for business also use it as their only social media platform. The C-suite members of your network scroll through the newsfeed in the evenings in the same way some people scroll through Instagram while waiting to pick up their kids from after-school activities.

Industry peers

Some of the best conversations I have on LinkedIn are with my fellow LinkedIn consultants. Strike that. *The* best conversations. We chat about updates, about clients gone wrong, about new features and how to use them. The same will apply for your industry.

A rising tide lifts all boats. When you engage with your peers, you learn together. Sometimes they may even send work your way.

More strategically, if someone in your industry is sharing some news about a product or service, and you comment in a thoughtful way on that post, their network will see your name and headline.

A word of warning: don't hijack your competitors' posts to try to win business. People will naturally follow you if you share valuable comments. They will see you when you try to swipe business from the person who wrote the original post. We all see you.

Thought leaders in your space

LinkedIn provides us with an easy way to keep up to date with what is going on in our industries. Social media is instant. Blogs and newspaper articles take longer to filter out. Following and connecting with thought leaders and influencers in your space not only keeps you up to date with emerging trends but it also helps your network to recognise you as up to date with your field.

Former colleagues

You may no longer work in the same company, or even industry, as your former colleagues, but who knows you better than they do in the professional space? They know your work ethic and your abilities, and could be a wonderful source of referrals for work.

I finished working in my health service role on a Friday and the following Wednesday was hired as a contractor to deliver a social media training workshop. The more I speak to small business owners, the more common I hear this is.

Industry journalists and LinkedIn News editors

Following or connecting with journalists can give you lots of fresh stories and content to share with your own network. You can also flip this around and, if you engage with their content regularly, you could become a source for their stories.

Case Study | **Oliver Banks, retail transformation expert**

Oliver Banks regularly posts content about the global retail industry. In 2022, he was contacted by a LinkedIn News editor and asked to contribute to a LinkedIn News article on the retail industry.

He obliged.

Building that connection with the News editor led to more opportunities and, in 2023, Oliver was named one of the UK Top Voices in Retail on LinkedIn.

Event organisers

There is a whole industry of people who organise speakers for conferences, webinars, podcasts and networking events. If you want to get booked, start connecting with the key people in your field who run events. Share content that showcases your speaking experience – and remember to deliver value, don't just blow your own trumpet.

Remember: people are watching you and reading your content, even if they never comment on any of it.

Suppliers and service providers

Very few of us work in a silo. Don't you need someone to provide the parts for your business? Maybe you want to outsource your content writing. Or you have zero skill in putting together graphics or PDFs.

If you work in manufacturing, this is a given.

Clients of ours who work in the automotive industry need multiple suppliers across their industry. By connecting with those suppliers, you can nurture relationships with them, as well as gain valuable insights into new trends and innovations in your supply chain.

As a potential provider to someone else, remember it is key to let your network know exactly what products or services you do supply. Keep yourself top of mind.

For example, my network is used to me sharing content that helps them with LinkedIn. I also want them to know we run a fully outsourced content management service that they can avail of, so the content we share needs to mention this service now and again. Without jumping into sales mode.

How can you do this?

Not like this:

Did you know we provide LinkedIn Company Page audits?
Here's how to book …

Like this:

When we were working with Acme Services recently to provide an audit of their LinkedIn Company Page, we found that more than half of their employees didn't have their Company Page correctly listed on their profiles.

Here's how to fix that:

A –

B –

C –

This post is helpful, but it also makes it clear to the reader that this is a service we provide: LinkedIn Company Page audits.

Mentors and coaches

Let's get something from our LinkedIn networks!

Following people who offer guidance on building your business or career, people who offer feedback and support, and people who inspire you in your own career path are great people to follow on LinkedIn.

You might even end up hiring one of them.

> **Top Tip** If you are looking for a coach or mentor, follow them for a while on LinkedIn and engage with their content before making a decision on whether they would be the right fit to work with you.

Alumni

Connect with alumni from your university or college. Not only do you share a common background, but sometimes they can open doors for you purely based on that connection.

You can use your university's page on LinkedIn to find alumni from your network and filter them by degree type and employment. There could be someone in there who can make a warm introduction for you into the industry you want to work in.

Recruiters and HR professionals

Even if you are not hiring, keep in touch with recruiters. Understanding what is going on within your industry can keep you up to date.

If you are looking for work, here are some top tips to keep in mind …

Top **Tip**

Top tips from career coach Sarah Burgess

Your LinkedIn profile picture and headline are two of the most important things you can optimise on your profile. These, along with your Experience section, are what LinkedIn recruiters look at when actively seeking candidates for potential job openings. Sarah recommends optimising these three sections of your profile if you're looking for new career opportunities.

She also recommends using the 'Open to Work' option if you're actively seeking a new role. Not only does this signify to recruiters that you're a potential candidate, but you can also write a message about the type of role you're interested in and why you're leaving your current role. You can also use the #OpenToWork hashtag, which will increase your posts' reach and show them to more people in their newsfeeds. Sarah also recommends tweaking your profile regularly.

Sarah is also a LinkedIn Top Voice. She was given this badge of honour in thanks for all the helpful tips and advice she shares on careers.

These tips are taken from an interview with Sarah for my podcast, which you can listen to here: www.louisebrogan.com/career-coaching-sarah-burgess/

Follow Sarah on LinkedIn for more tips like this: www.linkedin.com/in/sarahburgess

Cleaning up your network

Imagine if you only ever connected with people you wanted to on LinkedIn.

This won't be the case for most users. We are on this platform for B2B professional networking. When you go to an in-person networking event, there will always be that person you meet who, after five minutes of droning on at you about themselves, you can't wait to get away from. Well of course LinkedIn will be the same. But we have ways of dealing with this!

If you connect with someone and you find their content dull, boring or just plain uninteresting to you, you can unfollow them.

How different would this make your experience on the platform?

Top Tip You can choose to follow someone without connecting with them. And you can choose to unfollow someone without disconnecting from them.

Follow or connect?

When you see someone of interest on LinkedIn, you can do three things:

1. Click to follow their content.

2. Click to connect with them.

3. Click on the drop-down button beside the 'Follow/Connect' button and select 'Personalise Invite'.

The third option is my favourite. But if you only have the free version of LinkedIn, this choice is limited to five per month.

Let me explain the difference.

Follow

You are choosing to follow someone, which tells LinkedIn you'd like to see what they post.

- **Pros:** You can follow as many people as you want. These might be famous people, thought leaders, keynote speakers – maybe someone like Richard Branson.
- **Cons:** When you follow someone, they are not connected to you. They will not see any of your posts. They are notified that you are following them.

Connect

When you connect with someone, you are inviting them to join your network. If they accept, each of you will be able to see the other's posts.

Connect then unfollow

If you have people in your network you have connected with, and they are posting content you are not interested in, or posting too many things, you can choose to stay connected but to unfollow them. This means they will still be able to see your posts, but you will no longer be shown their posts.

Find out more

For a more detailed explanation of this, visit our YouTube channel, 'Raise Your Visibility Online', at www.youtube.com/@raiseyourvisibilityonline and search for 'follow or connect'.

Top Tip Your content gets more eyeballs when you have more connections engaging with you on LinkedIn.

What if your network is full of people you worked with years ago?

A lot of the workshops I deliver are to large organisations with people who may have been in the workforce for more than 15 to 20 years. If you created a LinkedIn profile when the platform first started (May 2003!) and did what was recommended over the years, you will have accepted everyone who sent you a connection request.

Do you ever see someone pop up on your newsfeed and you have no idea who they are or why you are connected to them? No? Maybe that's just me.

As well as unfollowing people in your network, you can 'train' LinkedIn to show you content from people you want to hear from, by engaging with their posts. Easy!

Will people know if you unfollow them?

Good news. Unless the person you are unfollowing is an online stalker, they will not know. No one is notified when you unfollow or disconnect from them.

Yes, it could get awkward if you disconnect from a colleague and they ask you about it in front of a room full of people.

This happened to me. Only I was delivering a training workshop. I swear the person had got me mixed up with someone else, as not only could I not remember ever meeting them, but also I had zero reason to remove them from my network. Awkward. So don't worry, it's already happened to me and I'm still standing!

You do want to get a good-sized network of connections on LinkedIn. If people visit LinkedIn once or twice a week on average, and you have 100 people in your network, when you post something, not many people are going to see it.

Even if you write a brilliant, thought-provoking piece, without other people engaging with your post, it won't get seen by very many people.

LinkedIn is just more interesting and fun when you build a network of value.

Chapter **6**

The algorithm

In this chapter:

Training LinkedIn to show you what you want to see

You can teach the LinkedIn newsfeed to show you the content you want to see. But to achieve this, the key thing you must do is start engaging.

What do I mean?

If you are on your LinkedIn newsfeed and you see a post from someone you find interesting, leave a comment. Next time they post, you are more likely to be shown their content.

Why is this?

LinkedIn wants its users (us) to stay on the platform longer. That means showing you posts from people you are interested in. How does it know you are interested in them? Because you already commented on or clicked on something they posted before. Simple.

How to stop seeing boring posts or people in your newsfeed

Likewise, if you see content from someone from your previous employer, who talks about issues you are no longer interested in, you can click the 'unfollow' button or choose to tell LinkedIn you are not interested. It will then stop showing you this type of content.

It doesn't take long to 'train' the algorithm to start showing you the type of content you want to see.

What is the algorithm?

Ahh, the multimillion-dollar question. All social media platforms run an algorithm to determine what and who we see on their platforms. It is the secret software code in the background that decides what you are shown. And who sees what you post.

The goal of the algorithm is to share relevant and interesting content with you that keeps you on the platform (or website) longer.

It is based on various things, including who you are following, the groups you are part of, the previous posts you have engaged with and your activity on the platform.

There are various guides out there to teach you how to 'beat the algorithm', but the idea here is that we grow a network who want to hear from us, we share posts, videos and updates that our network are interested in, and that we deliver something useful and valuable that keeps people coming back to find out more.

Keep it social

Another way to look at this issue is, are you using LinkedIn as a truly social platform? Ann Handley, chief content officer of MarketingProfs and Wall Street Journal bestselling author of *Everybody Writes*, says:

Top Tip

I'm always amazed by the number of people who treat LinkedIn as a broadcast channel. In truth, I'm also amazed by the people who treat any marketing channel as broadcast-only. But I digress …

What I mean by that: Stroll through the scroll of LinkedIn. Just randomly. Observe the people who post but don't engage in the comments. And observe those who are clearly robo-commenting, letting AI do the work for them.

Have we learned nothing since the dawn of SixDegrees, the first network that connected us all through the then-mewling newborn social web? (SixDegrees was the first network that connected one person's friends to another person's friends, and vice versa. It was the precursor to the kind of connections that are commonplace in modern social media.)

Too many of us forget about the 'social' and use it as pure 'media'.

Then we complain about engagement. Or we say LinkedIn 'doesn't work'.

My advice is to over-index on the social and less on the media. Why: Because you'll get the distribution (media) if you focus on the social. But the opposite isn't true. (Unless you're Richard Branson or Oprah.)

If you're reluctant to post, start with the social piece: Comment on posts by others. (Do not use AI to comment.) Add the media (publishing posts) later.

Build the network you want

If you want to use this platform and enjoy it, please build a network of people you are interested in. It doesn't all have to be strategic. If you hear someone on a podcast or read their book and you like it, connect, or follow them.

In between posting your own content and reaching out to potential clients, it makes LinkedIn more fun (yes, fun) when you see posts from people who are sharing stuff that you want to reply to.

Let's think of this like the lunch table at that conference you are attending. When you sit down with your sandwiches and coffee to take a break from listening to the speakers, don't you like to have a little small talk? I know I do. If it was all just business, I'd be exhausted!

The beauty of small talk, or water-cooler chat, is that it does, quite often, lead to contacts and referrals for business anyway. There's a reason why word of mouth is one of the most common ways people still get work in the 21st century. Humans like to talk, and we like to share good resources with good people.

Elizabeth Cook, a career and personal branding strategist from South Carolina, says one of her key benefits from using LinkedIn is her network:

Connection with others. I've maintained and deepened many relationships while meeting new people. This enriches my work experience tremendously and makes in-person networking more enjoyable too.

As Elizabeth points out, she is crossing the boundary between on- and offline – meeting people in real life who have followed her or met her on LinkedIn previously.

You tried this before and got nowhere …

Does all this sound familiar? You were building your network, posting updates to your newsfeed but getting nowhere?

Consider what type of content you were writing about.

Be honest with yourself. If you read the last five posts you put on LinkedIn, would you have found them interesting?

A common mistake on LinkedIn is to view it solely as a marketing tool for your business. Writing posts that talk about your products or service. Sharing how wonderful you are, and the last contracts you won.

Let's imagine for a moment this is all taking place at a business networking event.

You arrive at the event, get your coffee, and start talking to someone standing nearby. If you immediately launch into what your business is and how you work with people, how long do you think it will be until that person starts to find an excuse to move away?

People do not want to be sold to. Or broadcast at. If we want the nuts and bolts of how a service is delivered, we'll usually ask about it, or we'll Google something and read the article/blog/video that appeals to us most.

Social media marketing platforms are for building relationships with people. Yes, you want to market your products and services, but if you simply try to sell in your posts, no one will engage with them, and you will be losing leads.

And we don't want to be lectured at either.

There are a lot of building blocks to getting business from LinkedIn and they all need to have attention paid to them. If you have your profile optimised and you are building your network of people you want to be connected to, the next step is to create content that those people want to read/view/watch or hear.

Chapter **7**

Starting conversations: your LinkedIn content

In this chapter:

Encouraging engagement

The best way to create posts that get engagement is to view your posts as conversation starters.

Share an interesting piece of information that your network would find useful, and rather than treating this as a broadcast piece, think how you can turn it into a conversation. The simplest way to do this is to ask a question.

For example:

- You are a leadership coach.
- You want to sell your one-to-one leadership training programme.
- If you start promoting your programme, no one is going to respond or engage with you.
- So, consider the key questions people have when they find out you run leadership programmes. Take yourself back to the last sales call or event you attended – when someone asked you what you did, and you replied. What questions did they have for you?
- Thinking in this way gives you the basis for a post idea:
  - *Recently, during a leadership training workshop I ran, we were discussing Situation A.*
  - *I suggested they try this approach: Do A, Do B or Do C.*
  - *Have you tried any of these tactics and, if so, which one worked best for you?*

Ideally you will also be engaging with your own network on LinkedIn – you cannot post and run! By commenting on other people's content, you are also raising your own profile and attracting like-minded people who will start to click on your profile to find out more about you. The people who are the right fit will then either follow or connect with you. And if you are posting regularly, they will start to see your posts and engage with them.

Continue with the theme in your next post.

If people start to comment under your post, they are interested in this subject. Consider developing it out in the next post you create and include some of the insight from the people who commented on the initial post. Your network will see you as someone who is starting interesting conversations and will continue to want to engage with your posts.

What kind of content can you share on LinkedIn?

There are lots of different formats for posts to share on LinkedIn. You might be surprised!

First, you can simply write a post …

Written posts

If you are starting a conversation at an event, how does that look?

Let's pretend you have arrived at a whole-day conference for video marketing. You have met someone in the queue for coffee at the morning break. After you meet and say hello, introduce yourself. It could go like this:

I just attended Louise Brogan's talk about video marketing on LinkedIn.
Did you know that video on LinkedIn gets 40% more engagement than other kinds of posts?
People like to connect with others via video.
She said that you should keep the videos short and always add captions.
Have you used video on LinkedIn?

Let's break it down.

- Introduce the topic: what you are going to talk about.
- Share some useful information about that subject.
- Ask a question.

When you ask questions at the end of your posts, people are far more likely to respond to you. In the same way that if you walked up to someone at an event, made a statement and walked away – people do not want to be broadcast at. They want to have conversations.

> **Top Tip**
>
> No whingeing!
> Remember why you are on LinkedIn. Are you using it to become a thought leader in your space and to get known as an expert? Or are you using it to complain about things in your industry without sharing a useful way forward?

Include images

Posts with images work well on LinkedIn. Upload an image that is relevant to the post.

You don't need to stick to professionally taken photographs. Remember, this is your personal network in your professional career, so share images that reflect this.

When you upload an image, please ensure that you add alt text to the image – this helps screen-reading software to describe the image for people with visual impairments. I also recommend you tag the person/people in your image on the image rather than in the text of your post. It simply looks better online.

> **Top Tip**
>
> The golden rule of posting images is to post either one or three or more images. When someone uploads two images to a LinkedIn post, they sit parallel to each other and most of each image is sliced off at the sides.
> Multi-image posts are the most engaged-with type of post on Company Pages. This is because when people see a post with lots of images, human curiosity takes over and they click on the images to see them all.

Video content

I love it when our clients are up for creating video content.

There is no quicker way to grow the 'know, like and trust' factor on LinkedIn than video.

- **Credibility:** Video helps to establish you as an industry authority on LinkedIn – showcase your knowledge and share it!
- **Personal connection:** You will build stronger relationships with your audience by putting a face and personality to your brand, increasing the likelihood of attracting clients who resonate with your message.

- **Expanded reach:** Use video to reach a wider audience on LinkedIn, engaging both your network and potential clients, all while organically increasing your visibility.
- **Time saving:** Using video as your core content means you need an hour of your time each month to create all your content.
- **Consistency:** Set up a regular time each month to record your video for your posts. Consistently sharing video content with your audience nurtures them with valuable content and converts them into loyal clients eager to work with you.

My primary purpose on LinkedIn is connection. When posting, I'm trying to make people think, and hopefully elicit curiosity. This works so much better in person, and video is the next closest thing!

When I post videos, others really get a sense of who I am, how much I care and what it would be like to work with me.

Carol Wheeler, CEO of NopaLeadership

Documents or PDFs

Uploading a document to LinkedIn gives you a way to share a lot of your knowledge in a quick and easy fashion. The document in question doesn't need to be literally a document – it can be a PDF, slide show, presentation, company report, a white paper or even notes from your podcast.

How to upload a document

- Click on 'Create a post'.
- Select the 'Add a document' icon.
- Choose a file on your computer or upload one from the cloud (e.g. Dropbox).
- Add a document title.

Note that LinkedIn users who view your post will be able to download your document as a PDF file.

Top **Tip**

Top tips on sharing documents

- **Keep it short:** You can upload up to 300 pages, but best practice is between 8 and 25.
- **Use visuals:** When I wrote for Social Media Examiner,[12] the director of editorial, Lisa D. Jenkins, taught me that I should always have an image after every fourth paragraph as it makes the content visually easier to read. I still apply this to my own blogs and articles that are posted online.
- **Be conversational:** The best way to get your connections to engage with your content is to share an update that would sound similar if you were speaking in person to your network.

These are also known as 'carousel' posts on LinkedIn. They are very engaging because, in the same way people like to view multi-image posts, they swipe through each 'slide' or page of the document to get to the next one.

I recommend you use fewer words and more slides to get your message across. Think large, bold text that is easy to read.

You have the choice now to write something in the post about your document and add your hashtags before sharing the document post.

Written articles

LinkedIn articles vs LinkedIn posts: what's the difference?

While LinkedIn posts and status updates are limited to 1,300 characters, LinkedIn articles can be up to 125,000 characters, which gives you more opportunity to showcase your expertise and knowledge. Writing articles is also a great way to start conversations and raise your visibility on the platform.

When you open a LinkedIn article to read it on the desktop, an 'Articles' link to the person's byline appears. Clicking that link will display all the LinkedIn articles they've written. If you're viewing an article on the mobile app, simply swipe left to read the next article by that person.

By consistently writing articles using LinkedIn's Publishing platform, you'll build up your content library, and give users the opportunity to learn more about your business and build loyalty.

[12] *See: https://socialmediaexaminer.com/author/louise-brogan/*

How to choose a topic for your LinkedIn article

When you write articles on LinkedIn, you want to demonstrate your thought leadership, expertise and industry knowledge. News and updates from your industry make good topics to write about.

As mentioned earlier, you could also answer a question your audience has. What are the FAQs you get when you meet someone from your network? If you're a member of a Facebook group that contains your ideal clients, keep an eye out for the questions that are asked repeatedly. I use the Notes app on my computer to keep a list of ideas for blog posts and articles.

If one of your LinkedIn posts is getting a lot of engagement (comments and conversation) from your network, that might be a good topic for a long-form article.

Once you know what you want to write about, here's how to create your article on LinkedIn …

Write a new LinkedIn article

Start by going to the LinkedIn Home tab and clicking the 'Write article' link at the top of the page.

After you click this link, the LinkedIn Publishing tool opens. This is where you create your article.

Choose your headline

To add a title to your article, click the 'Title' field and type it in.

Choose a title that will grab users' attention in the feed and make them want to click through to read the article. Also think about what terms your ideal audience is searching for. 'How to …' and number titles (e.g. '7 Reasons to Start Writing LinkedIn Articles Today') typically perform well on the platform.

Format your article for easy reading

The next step is to format your article in a way that makes the information easy to consume.

Because we're bombarded with information and text online, it's best to use shorter text paragraphs interspersed with images. This approach makes your article easier to read, which is particularly important when people are consuming the content via the LinkedIn mobile app.

Adding subheadings, quotes, bullet points and bold type also improves readability.

How to format your article

The formatting toolbar at the top of the page lets you select Normal, Heading 1 and Heading 2 styles; apply bold, italics and underline to text; create bulleted and numbered lists; and use a quote style.

To link to an external source in the body of the article, first select the relevant text. Then click the 'Link' icon (at the far right of the toolbar), enter the URL and click 'Apply'.

Include images and video

Your article should have an image at the top, above your title. LinkedIn recommends an image size of 744 x 400 pixels. Free images can be sourced online at sites like Unsplash and Pixabay.

You should also include relevant images and video throughout your articles if you can.

To add an image or video, click on the plus sign at the left-hand side of your article.

You can also embed podcast episodes directly into your articles.

Include a call to action

Always include a call to action in your article. This could be asking people for their comments (a great way to spark conversation) or to get in touch with you. Links to your website, podcast or social media will work here too. The ideal is to encourage comments and when someone leaves a comment, make sure you reply to them.

Top Tip Once a post or article has received more than 10 views, you can access data on it.

Add hashtags

When sharing articles to your personal LinkedIn feed, adding hashtags can help you get more views on the link. LinkedIn encourages the use of hashtags when you create posts, and will suggest hashtags to use.

When sharing your article to the feed, tell your network why you're sharing it and add relevant hashtags to the post. The hashtags you use regularly will show up first.

Why you should reshare your LinkedIn article

Articles have a much longer lifespan than posts on LinkedIn. And while you can view the analytics for your posts for only 60 days, analytics for articles are available for two years.

You can give an article new life by resharing it via a LinkedIn post that directs users to it. I have several LinkedIn articles that still get comments a year or 18 months after they were published. How-to articles ('How do you write a good profile headline for LinkedIn?',[13] for instance) seem to perform best with my audience.

When you reshare an article to the newsfeed, focus on one main point or angle from the article. Then, a few days later, share your article to the newsfeed again, but this time focus on a different point.

To visualise this, if your article is about 10 reasons why someone should attend your Live event, list one or two of those reasons the first time you reshare the article. When you reshare it again a few days or even a week later, discuss some of the other reasons.

You'll see podcasters or bloggers using this tactic effectively on Facebook, X and Instagram. Simply adopt this same method to get more views and reads of your LinkedIn articles.

LinkedIn newsletters

What is a newsletter? Why would you write one? How can you become a newsletter creator on LinkedIn?

[13] *See: https://linkedin.com/pulse/how-do-you-write-good-profile-headline-linkedin-louise-brogan/*

The key difference between an article and a newsletter is that an article is standalone. For your CEO who does not want to commit to writing a regular newsletter, articles are perfect.

If you want to build a following of readers who can subscribe to your longer-form content, then I suggest you consider writing your long-form content as a newsletter.

When you publish your first newsletter, your whole network is invited to subscribe.

Today I have a network of more than 12,000 followers on LinkedIn and approximately 5,000 newsletter subscribers.

When you publish your newsletter, not only does it appear in the newsfeed and notifications of your subscribers but it also gets sent to their own email inbox. This is a powerful tool in your online marketing toolbox.

What is a LinkedIn newsletter?

A LinkedIn newsletter is simply a series of articles you will share on LinkedIn that your audience are able to subscribe to.

You can choose the frequency of your newsletter and the topic. LinkedIn recommends you write a newsletter based on a professional topic you care about.

Some example newsletter topics might be:

- D&I for industry
- advice for women returning to work
- blockchain news.

The difference between writing an article and creating a newsletter is that your subscribers will be notified when you publish your newsletter.

Anyone can discover, share or subscribe to your newsletter. They do not need to be in your LinkedIn first-connection network.

How do you access the newsletter feature?

If you have access to this feature, go to your LinkedIn newsfeed and click on 'Write article'.

Click on 'Create a newsletter' on the Publish menu.

To keep the platform professional, there are a few access guidelines. If you do not meet these criteria, you will not yet have access to publishing your own newsletter.

There are three key criteria for getting access to newsletters:

1. **Audience size:** LinkedIn's minimum audience for newsletters is to have at least 150 people in your network – followers or connections.
2. **You are already sharing original content:** In line with the criteria for LinkedIn Live access, the platform is looking for people who are already creating original content on LinkedIn. So simply sharing your blog or videos from elsewhere may not be enough. Upload your original video, create engaging posts, publish articles, etc.
3. **You abide by LinkedIn professional community standards:** Don't give access to someone else allowing them to log into your account, and avoid joining 'pods'. Share content that is useful and relevant to your professional life.

> **Top Tip** Start writing articles today, so that LinkedIn will recognise you as someone who shares original content and give you access to the newsletter feature.

Creating your first newsletter

Choose your title

What are you planning to write about? As this is your professional network, consider what you want to be known for. You can change your newsletter title later, but this is not recommended by LinkedIn.

What would appeal to your ideal reader? LinkedIn for Nonprofits has a monthly newsletter called 'Moving Forward'. A lot of the newsletters you will see on LinkedIn are simply titled with the company name. I suggest you try to come up with a more catchy name than that for your newsletter.

How often do you want to publish?

The choices are daily, weekly, biweekly (fortnightly) or monthly. You can change this option. The key is to pick a consistency you can stick to. Creating this as a task that someone in the company owns will help. Or you can outsource it to a company like ours.

Add your description

To encourage people to subscribe to your newsletter, consider the description. Who will it appeal to? Keep it simple!

> **Top Tip** To check which newsletters you are subscribed to, click on 'My Network' at the top of your screen. What titles and descriptions catch your eye?

Add your logo

Upload a logo for your newsletter – 300 x 300 pixels in size. This can be added or replaced later.

Invite your network to subscribe

When you publish your first newsletter, you can invite your whole network to subscribe to it. You are also able to share your newsletter and of course use other methods to invite people to subscribe, e.g. your email newsletter and other social media channels.

Email and push notifications are sent to all your newsletter subscribers once you hit publish on your next newsletter.

Writing your newsletter: best practice

Now you are ready to publish your newsletter.

Give each newsletter a title that will attract your subscribers to read it. Add a cover image – 744 x 400 pixels is the recommended size.

The structure of writing your newsletter is like that of writing an article. Key tips are to:

- write in short paragraphs and give valuable content – your readers will not be interested in fluff, unless you are a pillow manufacturing expert

- add images and/or links to video content
- format with bullet points and headings
- end your newsletter with a question to your reader, to engage them – ask them to subscribe and share, if relevant.

You'll find more useful information in this article: 'How to write LinkedIn articles that people will read and share'.[14]

If writing is not your thing, feel free to reach out for help – we can write your newsletter for you and all you need to do is hit publish.

Collaborative articles

What are collaborative articles and how can you contribute to them?

These are articles created by AI and published by LinkedIn. Experts are then invited to contribute their own real-life experience and expertise to the articles.

This is a pretty nifty idea – there are articles in several different topic areas – for example, finance, content creation, marketing and sales. You can find one that applies to your area of expertise and start adding in your thoughts.

Should you consider spending time on collaborative articles?

I think it's worth testing out for yourself. As with many aspects of LinkedIn, it helps you stand out from the crowd and raises your profile above those of your peers.

[14] *See: https://louisebrogan.com/how-to-create-linkedin-articles-that-people-will-read-and-share/*

Chapter **8**

Top tips on creating and sharing content on LinkedIn

In this chapter:

Creating content that people value

It's not me, it's you.

When you create content for LinkedIn, do you think about how it is received?

Are you delivering valuable content to your network that they want to read/watch/listen to? Or is it all The Me Show?

Have a look at the most recent 10 posts in your LinkedIn newsfeed. How many of your network shared a post that delivered actual value to you?

Does your newsfeed look like this:

- Sign up for **my** webinar.
- Listen to **my** podcast.
- Here's **my** gorgeous baby [not that I don't love baby photos].
- Here's an award that **I** won.
- Here's a sketch **I** found online that made me laugh.
- **I, I, I, me, me, me ...**

Be honest. How much do you want to read about how wonderful/amazing/inspiring everyone else is?

Remember the last bore you met at an event? They came up to you and talked all about themselves. The book they wrote. The holiday they are planning to take. The time they went to Buckingham Palace. (OK, so I did go to Buckingham Palace on an invitation to meet King Charles and yes I posted about it on LinkedIn – you would too if you had been there.) You walked away and thought, please let that person not be sitting beside me at lunch.

What about flipping it?

Could you write about how to help your network? Next time you write a post, stop yourself from talking about yourself. Turn it around. Write it to help your reader. Stop with the 'I' and start with the 'you'.

Human beings want to know what you can do for them. Yes, your friends will celebrate your wedding, promotion, sales, new baby. Of course they will. But are you also including posts that help them?

Are you a legal consultant? When was the last time you shared a post that gave some legal tips?

Don't overthink this. By sharing helpful advice on your area of expertise, your network will start to see you as the expert in your field. They will start to refer people to you.

What happens next?

When you consistently share valuable content on LinkedIn, people start to reach out to you directly. Maybe to connect with you, and – eventually – to work with you.

Take a notepad and start writing down ideas about what you can share on LinkedIn that will help your network.

What do you want to be known for?

Write your post and then check it for the number of times you say 'we' or 'me' or 'I'.

Now rewrite it to your reader.

Create a stage for your peers

If you can create a platform to let others shine, you will be seen as the leader in your space.

You also get to be the one with all the visibility. Cunning and yet generous.

Imagine you are hosting your own business breakfast. The topic is 'Learning and development: latest changes in the industry'.

As the host, you invite three industry leaders to join the event and be part of a panel.

They bring their own audiences along. You will get the recognition as the person who organises and hosts these events. The conversation starter. This is an easy way to build up your reputation and get known within your industry.

On LinkedIn this could look like a post, or even a LinkedIn Live event where you are the host and your guests are the panel.

Start simply. If you write a post about the latest changes in L&D in your industry, because you have been building a network of value that includes your peers, and you are posting consistently on the topic, you will build a following.

Sharing a post like this, with a question at the end, will encourage your peers to comment. The post can become a real conversation within your industry on LinkedIn. And you will be seen as the person who is leading this conversation.

If you are ready to move to the next level, why not consider hosting a LinkedIn Live event.

How to host your own LinkedIn Live event with others

We hosted a live stream with three members of a client team.

I set up the live stream, created an event on our LinkedIn Company Page and invited three members of the senior team as speakers. We then all invited members of our own personal network to attend the event.

In this way, the three team members are getting a chance to showcase their knowledge and expertise on LinkedIn. Plus, my company can then take that video recording and create multiple pieces of content from it for our clients.

Think about one 40-minute live recording.

You can create a blog post, a newsletter, clip out some short-form video, repurpose the content into carousel posts and clips for future written posts …

One video can create a whole month's worth of content. What a wonderful thought!

This is exactly what our agency does to help our clients.

On the day of the live stream, as the host of the event, I also got visibility in front of my client's network. Which is an industry we would like more business from. Everyone wins!

Respond to every comment

The third tip on making the most of your LinkedIn content and conversations is to reply to each comment. But, as your presence grows on LinkedIn, this can become more challenging.

John Espirian, self-described LinkedIn nerd and head of the Espresso+ community of LinkedIn aficionados says he aims to reply to every comment:

I've built a personal brand around being 'relentlessly helpful', and part of that involves making sure that people feel listened to, included and helped in the conversations that take place online. Because of that, I'd never knowingly ignore comments from people who engage with what I put into the world. No comment left behind!

If John can do this with a network of 46,000 followers and counting, then you can too.

Keep your network warm

You work hard to build up a network of value on LinkedIn. Each person who accepts your connection request is doing so because they feel you are going to share valuable content with them.

Comment on their posts

If you comment on someone else's post, they are more likely to engage with yours.

Share useful resources directly with them in the direct messages. Don't spam though!

Maybe tag them in a post you think they would like to read.

This could be your own post or something else written by someone in your industry.

Here's a story from Fiona Walsh, a client who worked with me on building out a whole LinkedIn strategy, about how she won 50,000 euros' worth of business through one LinkedIn post.

Case **Study** | How one LinkedIn post led to 50,000 euros' worth of work

Fiona Walsh is a PowerPoint expert who worked with me on her LinkedIn profile and strategy a few years ago.

She had recently delivered three workshops for a national organisation in Ireland. Her goal was that this would lead to more work that same year.

The organisation booked Fiona for a couple of two-hour sessions on PowerPoint. At this stage, Fiona was a trusted provider and connected to the learning and development team.

Fiona saw a post from the organisation saying that it had just gone through a rebrand. She put a post on LinkedIn showing she had just done some similar work with another public services firm in Ireland, which was similar to what they were doing. She didn't refer to the client who had just rebranded, she simply shared a post demonstrating what to do when you do rebrand and how this can impact your Microsoft Office set-up.

Fiona takes up the story:

I was working with a client on branding, and shared a screenshot of the work I had done – applying the branding to Excel and Word and all the other Microsoft products. I shared a screenshot of the theme that you can then apply.

Within an hour, the L&D person I was dealing with (from the original client) had screenshotted my post and sent it to the comms director.

And the comms director came straight back and said, 'Oh yeah, we need to talk about training.'

So that's why I went up to Dublin and met with the comms team, and they hired me for a contract worth 50,000 euros. That's my wonderful story.

Why this works

Fiona has built up relationships with her ideal clients. She stays top of mind with them because she shares content they find interesting. Fiona sticks to her core topic of how to use MS PowerPoint. She is also following her ideal clients and their content on LinkedIn so she knows when they make any internal changes or have some news.

By seeing their post on a rebrand, she was able to share some content that stopped the team member in their scrolling, they saw a service they needed, and Fiona was hired.

Top **Tip**

You can follow people or pages on LinkedIn by 'ringing' the notification bell on their profiles so you never lose track of their posts.

Engage with their posts, connect with key members of the company and build relationships that can turn into opportunities.

Chapter **9**

The COPE method of content creation

In this chapter:

We have created a way of working with our clients to make creating content easier for everyone. I call it the COPE method.

COPE stands for 'Create Once, Publish Everywhere' – an acronym I've borrowed from my old tech sector.

If you are going to spend time creating content, then I want you to be able to get as much mileage out of that content as you can.

Here's how it works …

Preparation/planning stage

Sit down with a pen and paper and work out what you want to share online.

Who is your ideal client? What are their issues? How can you help them?

Ideally the content will lead your ideal clients directly to a product or service that answers that problem for them.

For example:

- Lucy is a coach who works with senior leaders who are suffering from stress and overwork.
- Lucy is selling blocks of coaching sessions and is hired by an HR department that wants to reduce stress in the workplace.
- Lucy should create content that shows how productive team leaders can be when they are managing their workloads and reducing stress.
- Lucy should not create content that recommends yoga and taking long holidays to help with stress. Unless she is going to start a yoga retreat!

Ideally, you want to come up with six core topics. Then divide those core topics into four key questions. That gives you 24 posts. If you want to post twice a week on LinkedIn, you now have the basis for the next three months' content.

Now you have an idea of what you are going to talk about on LinkedIn. The next step is to create your pillar content. A pillar piece of content is one main piece that you can then chop up into many pieces.

Creation stage

Create one key piece of content to answer those questions. This could be video, a podcast or even a written article. The beauty of this method is that it doesn't matter what you start with. The aim is to repurpose that one piece into as many other pieces of content as you can.

Let's take a video ...

Record yourself answering the key questions you have on the topic. You will need a webcam or phone camera, a microphone and a bit of practice.

The resulting video is your core piece of content.

We love recording video content with our clients. I get to hang out with the client for an hour, ask them questions that they are very comfortable answering, and then we take that one core video and create multiple pieces of content from it.

Repurposing stage

There are lots of ways to repurpose this content. Here are a few suggestions ...

- **Writing:** Take your video and use software to produce a transcript. Use the transcript as the basis for a blog post and/or your newsletter. Upload your blog post onto your own website and embed the video into the blog for extra SEO (search engine optimisation).
- **Audio:** Download the audio to edit it and create a podcast episode.
- **Short-form video:** Edit the video into multiple short clips to repurpose across your social media accounts. Bear in mind that different accounts will prefer landscape or portrait video.
- **Images/graphics:** Take key points from the transcript and make a 'quote' image to share on social media.
- **YouTube video:** Now that you have a video, why not also post it onto your new YouTube channel? You will have to consider thumbnails, titles and YouTube descriptions – this could be the advanced level of your repurposing.

Analytics stage

How do you know if what you are doing is worth it?

You must get comfortable with some data. Social media platforms, Google Analytics, the number of messages, emails and leads who sign up to speak to you. Measure them all.

Check the analytics on your social media posts and the number of people who visit your website. Which format works best for you?

Your audience will prefer to engage with you in different ways. For example, I prefer to read articles, whereas others will prefer to learn from watching a video or listening to a podcast.

Reuse, recycle and repurpose

When you create content that explains what you do and how you do it, you can reuse this content again in the future. Keep the content you create filed away, and reduce future effort by reusing it. If the thought of this fills you with dread, invest in working with a virtual assistant to help you get organised.

Top Tip

When you create your content, use file names that are easy to organise and find in the future. For example:

- VID_LinkedInPages_March2024
- AUDIO_LinkedInPages_March2024
- BLOG_LinkedInPages_March2024

Chapter **10**

Following up with people

In this chapter:

The fortune is in the follow-up

As all good salespeople will tell you, the fortune is in the follow-up.

If you are using LinkedIn to grow your business, how do you get those connections and conversations to turn into actual leads?

This is one of the reasons I am such an advocate of connecting with a message. Once you start off with a message, you are speaking to your network on a one-to-one basis.

If you can, send a message when you connect with someone.

If you are on the free version of LinkedIn, we have a workaround:

- Send the connection request.
- When the person accepts your invitation to connect, you can now send them a personal message.

> **Top Tip** Did you know you can send video and audio messages, as well as attachments and documents, in your messages?

Don't jump the gun

Imagine we met at a conference. We said hello, and had a little chat about business and life. If you then handed me a 30-page brochure about your business and services, how do you think this would turn out?

Probably not well!

Unless … I asked you about your products and services. In that case, then I feel it is perfectly normal for you to offer to send me your brochure.

Notice I said 'offer' …

Your messaging strategy should be the same.

Connect with someone. Have a short conversation. Don't overwhelm them. Usually asking someone about themselves is a good idea. If that person then makes an enquiry about what your company does, offer to send them some more information.

Be prepared! Can you send them a link to your website? Maybe you have a YouTube channel. Or perhaps a nice five-page PDF outlining what you do and who you work with.

You could offer to have a call with them to discuss things.

If you want to move a little quicker than this, then if the person has messaged you a few times, you could offer to send more information before they ask. For example, 'We have worked with some other [insert the person's industry/job] recently. Would you be interested in having a look at the results?'

They can only say no. Or not right now.

Have you ever walked into a shop with the intention of buying something in the future and a salesperson puts you off straight away?

I have. I want to have a look around. If you come up to me and ask if I need some help, I will always say no.

Recently we bought a new sofa. We only intended to have a look.

We went into the sofa showroom. A salesperson came over after about two minutes to ask if we needed any help or were we just looking around. I said we were happy to look. She pointed out that she'd be nearby if we needed anything, and just to let me know they were hosting an Easter weekend sale.

We looked around. Sat on a few sofas. Lingered a bit.

The salesperson came back over to check on us. And to let us know that the sofa we were sitting on was on clearance. And to call her if we needed anything.

Ten minutes later we were on our way out and we spotted a sofa we really liked.

We sat down again!

This time no one came near us.

We chatted about the sofa for a minute or two and I said to my partner, I think we should ask about this one.

I looked over, and there was the salesperson. She was about 20 metres away. Not even looking at us. Next thing I know, she glances over, I give her a nod and she comes over to speak to us.

Thirty minutes later we had bought a new sofa. Zero sales pressure. Just checking in to see if we needed anything. We were obviously interested in a sofa that day.

On LinkedIn, what is the equivalent?

Someone connects with you. You have a few messages back and forth.

Nothing happens for a while.

Three days later, you see the person has been looking at your profile. Hmm. Maybe they are considering your services.

I suggest you click on their profile and see if they have posted anything recently. If they have, leave a comment.

Then send them a new message. If they posted, this is easy, as you can relate your message to their post.

If, like most people on LinkedIn, they haven't posted anything recently, this can be a little trickier.

Depending on what you have been sharing on LinkedIn, could the post you have written be of interest to this person? If so, why not send it to them in a message with a short note – 'thought you might be interested in this'.

Remember, this is LinkedIn. It is a social media platform you are using to build your business. It is OK to offer your services and share your content!

If this makes you feel a bit icky, what about opening the conversation up again?

I create posts that share tips on how to use video on LinkedIn.

I know from following my data that certain people have clicked on links in my newsletter about our video services. When I see that, I reach out to those people on LinkedIn and check in with a quick message.

This is a little easier than sending them an email. After all, social media is a more casual place to hang out, right?

What's the worst that can happen?

They ignore you. Ghost you. Remove you from their network. Leave your email list.

Guess what? They were never going to buy from you in the first place!

Now you have more time to spend with the people who are potential clients.

Chapter **11**

Scenario: Thinking of LinkedIn as an in-person event

In this chapter:

My favourite way to explain how LinkedIn works is to reimagine it as your industry conference. The one you go to each year, where you meet the people you do business with, hopefully win new business and generally connect with your network in person. Maybe you even pitch to speak on stage or invest in a sponsor booth at this conference.

Let's explore this analogy …

Finding and signing up for an event

Recently, I met Lindsay at Social Media Marketing World in San Diego. This is a two-day conference preceded by a pre-conference day, where organised workshops and networking are available.

The organisers of this conference had sent out an email to invite women who were travelling to the event to a special women's networking breakfast. As I was attending on my own, I was delighted to have something arranged by the conference that I could kick off the event with. I registered before I even got on the plane.

The LinkedIn equivalent of this could be you finding an event hosted by a Company Page and signing up for it. When you do this, you are sent a calendar reminder by LinkedIn that goes into your own personal calendar, whether that is MS Outlook, Google or iCal.

The personal profile

I arrived at the conference, registered and headed to the women's networking breakfast. I met Lindsay when I arrived, as she sat down at the table I was at, and we got chatting.

After speaking about San Diego, the conference and who we were excited to see speaking, I asked Lindsay about herself and her job. Turns out she was a sponsor of the event. After the breakfast event, we swapped details and I went on to a workshop.

In this story, meeting Lindsay at the breakfast event would be the equivalent to you 'meeting' someone in the comments of a LinkedIn Event. Or maybe you are reading an interesting post from a thought leader in your industry and you spot someone who writes a thought-provoking comment under that post, and you like what they have to say.

You head over to look at their profile and maybe connect with them.

You (ideally after reading this book) send them a private message to say hello.

The Company Page

Later that day I was walking past the sponsor booths when I spotted Lindsay, so I headed over to say hello. I met her colleague, found out more about their company and what its products and services were, and walked off with more information about their business.

As you are interested in the work that this new person you have met does, the equivalent back on LinkedIn would be to pop over to check out their Company Page.

This is where you should be able to read more about the business and its products and services, and to see who else works there. What kind of impression do you get from the business?

In a busy online world, the chances of me coming across a page like this by accident are minimal. Yes, some of my network might already be following it, which would make it more appealing to me – but only once I had 'met' Lindsay would I have gone to check out her business's Company Page.

The key reason I went to see this page was because I'd met one of the business's team.

When I connect with someone new on LinkedIn and I am genuinely interested in their services, I always go to see what is happening on their Company Page. At an in-person event, the equivalent would be continuing the conversation at the sponsor booth or merch stall or website.

When I meet someone on LinkedIn, I might click through to their website too, see who else works there and what kind of stuff they are sharing, but the reality is that I am unlikely to visit a website from a personal profile – I am already on LinkedIn, so it is an easy click-through to check out their Company Page. Just like it is easy to walk across the hall to visit the sponsor booths at an event.

How your people drive traffic to your Company Page

On LinkedIn, your team are your biggest asset – just as they would be if they were attending a conference.

At conferences, you notice the people who are wearing their company branding. Maybe it's a hoodie, maybe a cap. It is an easy way to get more visibility for your business brand. On LinkedIn, those people will no doubt have the company logo and branding all over their personal profiles.

The people your team meet and connect with, the conversations they have, and their level of knowledge on how LinkedIn works, all have an impact on the visibility of your business on this platform.

And if you are a solo entrepreneur, the same applies to you.

Your Company Page represents your brand. Use it to share your products and services. What your company does. What sort of company it is. What you stand for.

If you have a team, train them to grow your business on LinkedIn.

Think of your Company Page as your merchandise stall

For another way to look at this, I'll turn to my Springsteen analogy …

Bruce Springsteen is famous in his own right. But behind the man is the whole business. We have the musicians (the E Street Band), the management, the tour operators, the vinyl, the T-shirts, hoodies, caps, badges, and so much more.

While Bruce is very clearly the frontman, the whole thing works because there is a business operating.

Think of your Company Page as being like your merchandise stall at the next concert you go to. You 'meet' singers on the radio or a music app (depending on your age!) and when you hear someone you like, you check out their back catalogue, find out if they are touring, or even buy their vinyl.

The key to all this is that the easiest way to bring attention to your business – and therefore your Company Page on LinkedIn – is to engage with other people as your personal profile on LinkedIn. Everyone in your team is able to invite their personal professional network to follow your Company Page. After all, we only go to the merchandise stall at the Springsteen gig because we love the music he creates.

Now let's imagine a different scenario …

The silent scroller

I walk into the business breakfast in San Diego. I sit down with my coffee and watch all the other people chatting. I don't speak to anyone. I don't meet Lindsay.

I leave having enjoyed watching everyone else interact, but I don't have any new contacts. I certainly don't head over to the sponsor booth later that day to chat with my new friend.

Unfortunately, this is what happens with most LinkedIn users.

You pop onto LinkedIn with your cuppa to see what is happening. You scroll through some posts. You read a few articles.

You never post. You don't leave comments. You certainly don't meet a new contact and have conversations with them. And so no one ever visits your profile or your Company Page.

Let's flip that narrative …

Reimagining the LinkedIn platform

Let's take our analogy a little further in terms of how we approach LinkedIn to make it more accessible.

If your personal profile is the LinkedIn equivalent of you meeting people in real life, and your Company Page is the equivalent of a sponsor booth at a conference, what else can we expect at this in-person event?

What makes a good conference? I think there are several factors to take into consideration: the hosts, speakers and sponsors, and of course the organisation running the event, the opportunity to network, your fellow attendees, the 'rules' – are people pitching you from the stage? Let's hope not.

Let's break these down.

The hosts

Microsoft owns LinkedIn. It would be fair to suggest that it is a pretty well-respected corporation. One of the reasons professionals spend time on LinkedIn is that those who make up the network are, overall, respectful to one another. My own theory on this is that if you are on a social network where your colleagues and employers are present too, you will probably behave professionally.

If you were to attend your industry conference with your team, you'd show up as though you were ready for work, both in terms of what you are wearing, but also in terms of your attitude. It should be no different on LinkedIn.

You show up as your personal profile. You (hopefully) don't hit the bar in your shorts and T-shirt. Or maybe you do! If that is how you do business offline, then your LinkedIn would reflect that. But maybe those brands are hanging out on Instagram.

The speakers

Let me introduce Bill.

One of my network, Bill Callahan, self-described experienced financial crime and anti-money laundering expert, has built up a network of law enforcement, anti-money laundering, financial crime, cybersecurity and related businesses. When Bill posts, his network engage. If you check out his profile,[15] look at his posts and his activity – you will see so many frank and open discussions around financial fraud, cybercrime, and so on.

Each person has the choice to build the network they want on LinkedIn. Everyone has a unique experience with their time spent on LinkedIn. I have very

[15] *See: https://linkedin.com/in/william-j-callahan-iii/*

little experience or knowledge of Bill's world and so I generally don't engage with his content. We did connect over podcasting, though, and luckily for me Bill likes learning about LinkedIn, so he tells people in his network to follow me. I am one of his 'speakers'.

Organisation

A well-organised conference is an enjoyable experience. From arriving on time, having an agenda, well-thought-out speakers and breakout sessions, to the food and location – a good organiser will have thought of everything.

How is LinkedIn any different? You find your newsfeed down the centre of your LinkedIn screen. It suggests people for you to follow. The algorithm serves up content based on your previous activity on the platform.

It removes 'bad apples' from the platform. You can report someone's post as inappropriate, or you can give feedback on content that you may not want to see in your feed. Your reason for not wanting to see certain content could be simply because it is irrelevant to you – like leaving a boring talk at a conference and heading to a different room to see who else is speaking.

With some in-person events, if you want to speak to the organisers to complain about something, it can be a little hard to get hold of them. After all, they are running the event! LinkedIn should not be similar, but the truth is, with a billion members, yes, it can be challenging to get hold of someone to share your complaint with. In my experience, you usually get a response within a day or so.

Top Tip

To reach someone in the LinkedIn team through chat, click on your 'Me' drop-down menu at the top of the screen, then click 'Help'. In the popup that opens, click on 'Open Help in a new tab' and, at the bottom of this new tab, you will – depending on your account access – find 'Start chat'. If you can't see this option, you can still use the search box to find the answers to most questions.

If you are not able to reach someone in the LinkedIn team through chat, sometimes it can be quicker to send them a message via X!

Opportunity to network

You may not actually be attending an in-person event to hear the speakers. Maybe the topics are at a level you have already passed, but you know that your peers will be in attendance too.

There is a social media conference I plan to attend in the UK later this year. I believe that most of the speakers will be sharing content that I am already familiar with. However, the price of the ticket is worth it to me, as there will be hundreds of my peers attending. We will have the chance to meet for coffee, attend unofficial meet-ups and catch up in person with business friends from all over the UK who will all be in the same city at the same time.

In the same way, you may not be learning anything new or groundbreaking from the post you just read on LinkedIn, but in the comments you see others who work in your field.

In the spirit of collaboration and community, these are the people I suggest you connect with and build relationships with. Plus, by commenting on the content posted by speakers like that, you are also supporting them. Cheering them on from the front row of the conference, so to speak.

Finding your ideal client in someone else's talk

A wise man once gave me this advice. If I were to attend his conference in person, the biggest tip he had to share with me was that I should attend the LinkedIn talks. Not because he felt I needed to learn from my colleagues. But because the room would be full of people who wanted to learn how to use LinkedIn.

Genius.

If you want to find people who are asking questions about the area you provide services in, where are you going to find them? At a workshop or talk about that area!

When I attended the conference where the LinkedIn talks were taking place, but I wasn't a speaker, the person speaking on the stage was very definitely seen as the expert. I was able to see what questions the audience had and to take note of those questions to help figure out what content I could create to raise my own profile.

Translating this to LinkedIn, I am not suggesting you hijack your competitors' posts to try to show up as the expert in the comments. But I am asking you to take note of the questions that people post to that person and add them to your own list of ideas for content to share with the network.

What if you become the expert?

My client Fiona Walsh, who we first met in Chapter 8, is a PowerPoint expert. I suggested she create a 'platform' that all the other PowerPoint experts could contribute to by writing posts that start conversations around PowerPoint and its features. The LinkedIn network did not disappoint. When Fiona writes posts about tips and methods for improving your PowerPoint slides, her 'competitors' add their own thoughts.

Fiona has created a stage for others to share their thoughts and wisdom. In doing so, she is seen as the leader of these discussions.

I can imagine some of you thinking, why would I want to create a platform for others to win business from my network? Let's reset that mindset for a moment. There is more than enough business to go around for everyone.

Can you imagine if there was only one LinkedIn trainer/speaker in the world? Or in your city? How on earth would they be able to serve all the potential customers? I'd rather we build a network of people who are happy and willing to share.

The attendees

This leads us to the attendees. As discussed earlier, the other attendees are your potential clients. They also want to learn about the topics being discussed on stage. Look at who is interacting with the speakers in your industry and connect with them. Maybe you are sitting next to someone and they make a comment about the talk you just heard.

When I attended Social Media Marketing World in San Diego, I went along to three of the LinkedIn talks. They were excellent, as I'd hoped they would be.

I sat beside a lady who turned out to be the marketing manager of a start-up in California. She remarked that they had invested in some training for their company and hired a well-known LinkedIn trainer.

I asked how it went, and she told me that overall it was useful, but that it was lacking in a particular area she was interested in. Rather than dive in to offer my services, I took note of what she said. And now I am creating content around that area because I see others are not focusing on it.

Likewise on LinkedIn, I recommend you do not leap into the comments to offer yourself up as a replacement for the person who is the original poster. I don't even think you should DM commenters with your services. But you could connect, and when you create content that answers the questions they were asking, you will be on the right path and you will have kept your integrity intact.

If that goes against your way of working, this may not be the right book for you!

Making introductions

One of the best ways to meet people in business is to be introduced by someone you already know. LinkedIn is no different.

Imagine attending an event with 500 people. You walk in the door with the intention of connecting with five to ten potential clients. You head into the room for the next talk and see a business coach you have worked with. They are sitting with one of your target potential contacts. Why not head over and say hi? They should introduce you to this other person. If not, you could ask later if they wouldn't mind introducing you.

On LinkedIn, this is made relatively easy.

When you see a potential lead, you can check if you have potential connections in common. Unless the other person is 'hiding' their network, you are shown which connections you both have, right at the top of the personal profile on the Introductory Card. Why not ask a common connection if they can introduce you to the other person?

A three-way introductory message is a great way to meet someone on LinkedIn, as well as in person. Trust is a huge factor. Don't blow it!

To set up a three-way message, the other person clicks the little pen icon to send a message. In the window that pops up, you can add as many people as you want to the message chat. Ideally, if you are using this to introduce two people to each other, you will keep it short and simple.

Sales Navigator

If you have the Premium account Sales Navigator, this is made even easier, as LinkedIn will suggest people who can connect you to the lead you want to speak with. However, at the time of writing (October 2024) this service starts at $79 per month, and you can probably find the leads you want out on the 'main floor' that is your LinkedIn newsfeed rather than heading for the 'conference VIP room'.

Preparing for the event

Is this the right place for you?

When you choose a social media platform, what do you take into consideration? The people? The content? The network? The organisation that runs it?

All these same things apply to choosing an in-person event to attend.

You may have heard of the event from someone in your network, who suggested you'd enjoy attending. Or you met a colleague who is already a regular attender of a networking in-person event local to you, and you can see that they are winning business because of attending the event.

Is your LinkedIn account your own?

There is a difference between how companies perceive LinkedIn for their employees vs how you perceive it. Your personal profile is yours. Yes, you can attach yourself to your Company Page, but at the end of the day, when you leave that employer, you take your profile, your content and your network with you.

It's the same in real life.

Consider the business connections you make who invite you out for lunch when you are in their city. Maybe you have worked with mentors over the years who send you an article link because they think you'd be interested.

Does your activity on LinkedIn generate enquiries that lead to business for your company? All of this is connected to your personal profile and activity on LinkedIn. And is also what a lot of employers are afraid of! When you leave the company, those leads and connections go with you.

But if we all lived in fear of what might happen, then we'd probably never leave the house.

How can companies tackle this challenge?

If a company focuses on building its brand, and gives its employees material and content to share, then those employees will be amplifying the company's message. Most employees who are active on LinkedIn tend to be creating their own content and noise. What if you, the marketing manager, created content so good that most of your team used that content to share with their network? Wouldn't that be a better approach?

How to prepare for LinkedIn

When you are preparing to attend an in-person conference, there are several stages of preparation. Let's go through them …

First – deciding what event to attend.

Ideally if you are going to take time out of your busy week to attend an event, you will aim to go to something that will either (a) expand your knowledge or your network, or (b) be highly enjoyable.

LinkedIn is no different. By creating a network of people you want to connect with, who are sharing ideas and articles that you want to read, and stories you find engaging, you know you are in the right spot.

Second – as you leave your house to head off to the event, how are you set up?

I would imagine you are dressed to meet your professional network. You might have some flyers or marketing materials with you. You put your best foot forward.

In LinkedIn terms, I see this as you spending time optimising your personal profile. Dress it up. Make it look appealing to your ideal audience. (By appealing, I mean that you look like someone we'd want to do business with. This is not a dating site!)

Chapter **12**

Your LinkedIn profile

In this chapter:

Creating an engaging personal profile

Let's take it from the top …

Your Introductory Card

At the top of your LinkedIn personal profile, you have an Introductory Card. This is the rectangular area at the top of your profile with your name, photo, headline and employer. Think of this as the name tag you get when you register at an in-person conference. Only with a lot more information.

Images

There are many places to put images across your personal profile, but the absolute key one is your profile photo.

This image follows you around LinkedIn – when you post, when you comment, when you sign up for events, even when you send someone a message. Almost all the activity you have on LinkedIn includes your profile photo.

Your profile photograph should be a clean and clear recent picture of your head and shoulders. I recommend the photo should be of you looking at the camera, preferably smiling and looking approachable so that people will want to connect with you and reach out.

Some people have coloured rings around their profile photo. You can add these yourself or use the ones provided by LinkedIn – at time of writing, these are either to show you're hiring or that you are looking for a new job ('Open to Work').

Make sure that your profile photo is visible publicly so that if someone sees your comment on someone else's post, they can see your face and they're more likely to click on your profile to find out more about you.

Top Tip Have a recent headshot. If someone is to meet you in person, they would want to recognise you from this photo.

Background/cover photo

This is a space to include your branding – maybe have your logo, or images of you speaking on a stage. If you have an event or a book launch coming up, this space can be used to promote that event. You can change your background image as much as you want. People will only see it when they visit your profile – unlike your profile photo, which can be seen in multiple places.

Top Tip If you are managing a Company Page, create a couple of these branded images to share with your team. They can be used to increase the visibility of the company, as well as making it easy for your colleagues to include a background image on their personal profiles.

Your personal profile headline

A LinkedIn headline tells people in a short phrase or paragraph what you do and who you do it for. I see your headline as a way of attracting the right people to connect with you.

When you create posts or comment on other people's content, the network will see your profile photo, your name and your headline. Consider what keywords or phrases will attract the right kind of attention. For example, if you are a podcast editor for small businesses, please use that at the start of your headline.

If you don't add a headline, LinkedIn uses the role you have as your current job/position. That's why we see so many headlines like 'project manager' or 'accountant'.

Make sure your headline tells people what you do and who you do it for.

Contact information

Next is your 'Contact info' button. Here you can add in your phone number, your email and your websites.

You can include multiple websites. You can have a link here to your podcast website, for example, and your Twitter/X handle if you have one, and your birthday too.

I recently ran an experiment on my birthday, setting the details to make them visible to my network. I got about 250 messages from my network, which opened conversations with quite a few people who are good leads for me. Now, lots and lots of people in my network are not going to ever become clients or customers. And that's fine. But doing something like this does start a lot of conversations with people – it will really raise your visibility, which could lead to something down the line.

LinkedIn Premium profile options

If you invest in LinkedIn Premium services, you have the option to show a gold LinkedIn button on your profile.

There are different types of Premium account, including:

- **LinkedIn Business**
- **Recruiter**
- **Sales Navigator.**

For most of you, a 30-day trial of LinkedIn Premium will showcase what you can use it for. Personally, I like having access to information on who has viewed my profile, in case there is a nice lead showing up there. Premium also gives access to LinkedIn Learning, which is an excellent depository of training video content.

Some people have a blue LinkedIn button. These people have been anointed as LinkedIn Top Voices. This is a super-fancy title that is given to 10 people a year inside different industries – for example, Top Voices in sales or retail. This designation can bring you a lot of extra followers, and LinkedIn may (or may not!) share your content with its audience via the LinkedIn News team.

External links

One of the key reasons we use social media is to drive potential customers and clients to connect with us. Whether the next step is picking up the phone, writing an email, sending a WhatsApp or visiting your website, you want all your efforts to lead to sales or conversations.

There are a few places you can add external links on LinkedIn. Choose carefully and try to test out different options.

Here are some of the key places to add links:

- If you are a non-Premium account member, include your website address in the Contact info on your Introductory Card.
- You can also add clickable links in your Experience and Featured sections.

These links can be to any URL on the internet, and you can edit and change them as you wish.

Write something that will attract your ideal clients to click on the link – for example, a free resource available on your website.

Follower numbers

Try not to get too hung up on your network size or follower numbers. Building a network of value means that you get to curate who you connect with. I prefer having a network of people who share interesting posts and video content to building an enormous network of followers who are not terribly interested in interacting with my content.

You do have a minimum goal to aim for, though: more than 500 people. Once you have more than 500 people in your network, LinkedIn will change from showing the exact number of people you are connected to, to showing 500+.

> **Top Tip** A word of caution: do not try to build up to more than 500 people in your first few weeks. Take your time and send connection requests to people you have met, interacted with, or who you find interesting. In this way, you will enjoy meeting new people and building relationships rather than opting for 'bigger is better' network building.

Public profile and URL

Have you got a LinkedIn URL yet?

The easy way to share a link to your LinkedIn profile is by creating a personal profile link. On desktop, click on your 'View Profile' button and navigate to the top right-hand side of the screen. You will see a clickable link to edit your 'Public profile & URL'. When you click on the pencil icon, a new screen will appear. In this screen you get a preview of how your profile looks to people on the internet who are not connected to you.

The key things to change here are the URL for your profile and your profile privacy settings. This is up to you, however I recommend you set your profile photo to public. This means that, when someone who is not yet connected to you sees your comments on LinkedIn, they will now see your name, photo and headline. Before, they may only have seen a grey circle where your face should have been.

About

Next, we have the About section, and this is what I call the really heavy lifting area of your profile.

Once people have clicked on your name and your headline, they'll be scrolling down through your profile to find out more about you, and the About section is a real opportunity to win those people over.

When I host VIP sessions with clients,[16] this is definitely the place where we spend the most time, because most people have written just a few lines about who they are and what they do.

What to include

When you are chatting with someone at an in-person event, what is more appealing to you: they ask you all about you and your business, or they talk at you and tell you about themselves?

I thought so.

This section should be about your customers and your clients, what they're struggling with and how you can help them. So you want to make sure you've included what problems your current customers have that you help them with, how you can help your potential clients and customers, what services you provide or what products you have.

[16] *Find out more about these here: https://louisebrogan.com/linkedinvip/*

Call to action

Always end with a request to connect with you, whether it's to connect on LinkedIn, follow your LinkedIn, to send somebody to your website, your email address …

Whatever it is, make sure you invite people to reach out to get in touch with you.

Formatting your About section

One of the key things to consider is how you format your About section.

Have plenty of white space, so it is easy to read. LinkedIn doesn't recommend using any fancy fonts or formatting, as this is not inclusive. When someone uses a screen reader to 'read' the text, this type of text is not captured.

You can still create emphasis in this section by adding in emojis such as the red drawing pin or green tick/check mark. I use asterisks and equals symbols to create breaks on screen like this:

****

===

And I create breaks or sections by USING CAPITAL LETTERS.

Visit the About section of my own profile on LinkedIn to see this in action: www.linkedin.com/in/louisebrogan/

Adding skills to your About section

When you update your Skills section on LinkedIn, you are now able to check a box to say where those skills are used. You can also add your top five skills into your About section.

All these little extra steps will help you to get found by your ideal client when they are searching for someone with your skill set.

Services

If you provide services to other businesses – for example, coaching, consulting, podcasting – I recommend you create a Services page on your personal profile.

When you create a Services page, you can add up to 10 services, and people both in your network and those who are searching for the services you provide can request a proposal of work from you.

Featured

'Featured' is a section on Your LinkedIn personal profile where you can choose to share posts, links, videos or articles that you want to highlight.

What types of content can you put in your Featured section?

You can upload posts, articles, links to external sites and media. Reverting to our analogy from the previous chapter, of meeting someone at a conference, this could be the equivalent of the products and services you choose to feature at your sponsor booth. Or the deeper conversations you have with someone you have met before.

Experience

The keywords and content in your Experience section help people find you on LinkedIn for your current products or services. This section is where you add details of your current and former positions, as follows …

Add position

- Title
- Employment type
- Company name
- Location
- Location type
- Currently working
- Industry
- Description
- Skills
- Media

Repeat this for any past employment you wish to include, but note that when you are using LinkedIn for business, you do not need to include all the previous roles you may have had in your career.

I worked in several temp jobs when I was a student, for example, and these do not appear in my profile. Whereas the two corporate roles I worked in, as a software engineer and an ICT project manager, do. The strategy behind this is to reflect to my potential clients that I have experience working in the corporate space.

Adding media to your Experience section

You can also add media here – for example, a link to a video or to your website – and it really pops off the page.

Education

This is where you add details of your education. If you went to university, add that information. When you do this, make sure you select the actual university from the drop-down box, so that its logo appears in your Experience section, and up on the Introductory Card at the top of your profile. (You can also choose not to highlight your university on your Introductory Card.) If you don't use the link to the university in the drop-down, then it just shows like a little grey box, which doesn't look quite as good.

Top Tip

If you have more than one university qualification, you will need to choose which one to display on your Introductory Card. Does Harvard Business School top Yale? You decide!

Licenses & Certifications

Next comes the Licenses & Certifications section. Here's the place to add in any that you have.

There is also a Volunteer section, so remember to fill in these seemingly small sections. If you have been a volunteer, add that in – every little helps on your profile.

Someone else may also like the cause or charity you worked with, and it can become something you connect over.

Skills

Check your Skills section and any related endorsements. Run through all the skills you have listed to make sure they are skills you still use now, not just in the past, and your network will start to endorse you for your skills.

Did you know that the Skills section of your profile is how to show up in the LinkedIn search results?

On your personal profile, scroll down to the Skills and endorsements section.

On your LinkedIn profile, you can add up to 50 skills. LinkedIn will show your top three skills to the viewer. To see more than the top three, the person viewing your profile must click on the 'Show more' link that appears on-screen.

What are the LinkedIn skills categories?

There are five key categories of skills on LinkedIn:

- **Top Skills**
- **Industry Knowledge**
- **Tools and Technologies**
- **Interpersonal Skills**
- **Other Skills.**

You can add three 'Top Skills', which you can select yourself. If you don't select your own top three, LinkedIn will select them for you at random.

Top **Tip** When looking for skills to add, start typing your first word slowly and LinkedIn will auto-complete the options.

Recommendations

Try to get into the habit of asking customers, clients, people you've worked in teams with, for recommendations of your products and services. Likewise, think about recommending other people. One of the great things about LinkedIn is that it is a massive social networking site. So you want to network with people. Be generous with your comments and your messages, and your support of other people.

How to ask for recommendations

You can only ask for a recommendation from someone who is directly connected to you on LinkedIn. Which makes a lot of sense. If I want to know more about the person speaking on stage at the conference I am attending, I'd rather hear from someone who has already worked with them or known them a while.

Giving recommendations

It is generous to give recommendations. Both in real life and online. Taking time out of your own schedule to recommend someone else reflects well on you.

A tip I picked up from a fellow LinkedIn podcaster, Mark Williams, is to check out what recommendations someone has given to people within their network.

This tells you what personality traits appeal to the person you are looking at.

For example, if they recommend someone based on their professionalism and speed of execution, you know they are attracted by those skills, so you could emphasise them in your language when you speak to or message them.

Chapter **13**

How to amplify your profile with video

In this chapter:

Did you know you can add video to different places in your personal profile? The key areas for this are your Featured section and your Experience section. We'll discuss this in the second part of this chapter.

It used to be the case that you could add video to your personal profile photo, but that option was removed. Maybe it will return when LinkedIn's new short-form video service is rolled out.

Why does video work so well?

Before we discuss all the places you can use video, let me explain why it works so well.

When you watch a video, you are using two senses: hearing and sight. As humans, we connect with people when we see them and hear them speak. It is easier to watch and listen to someone than it is to read something they have written.

When people speak, they pause in the right places, they place emphasis on words, and they can put emotion behind their words.

When you record video of yourself speaking into a camera, the viewer has the impression you are speaking directly to them.

Top Tip When recording a video, make sure you look into the camera lens, and not at your script or yourself!

Of course, you need people to turn the sound on for them to hear you, which doesn't happen much on LinkedIn.

I wanted to use the stat here that people connect 60,000 times faster with visuals than with text but as I was fact-checking, I found that, apparently, there is no scientific basis for this claim![17]

I do believe that people connect faster with images, though, and this is backed up by a study at MIT, described on the MIT News website in an article titled 'In the blink of an eye'.[18]

[17] *'The 60,000 Fallacy', PolicyViz, 17 September 2015. Available at: https://policyviz.com/2015/09/17/the-60000-fallacy/*

[18] *'In the blink of an eye', MIT News, 16 January 2014. Available at: https://news.mit.edu/2014/in-the-blink-of-an-eye-0116*

We are not neuroscientists though (well, I'm not anyway), so let's look at this another way ...

What makes video such an engaging tool?

Let's imagine we are back at our in-person conference.

You are passing by the sponsor booths, and you spot a company that sells a product you are interested in. Maybe it's an email marketing company.

You'd like some more information on the company's services, and the person at the booth looks friendly enough. Maybe they have some of those free chocolates you love on the stand ...

You head over to the booth. There are a few ways you can get the information you want:

- Speak to the person running the booth.
- Eavesdrop on the conversation the salesperson at the booth is having with someone else.
- Pick up a flyer or leaflet.
- Watch a screen demo they have set up at their booth, if they have one.

Which of these options do you think will engage you the most?

I would imagine speaking to the person. But when I have seen demonstration videos at a booth, I find they offer a much quicker way to find out if this is the right tool or company for me.

Video serves the same purpose on LinkedIn.

When you go shopping, do you prefer to walk around a shop and have a look at things first, or do you speak to the salesperson who asks if you need anything?

I think the answer depends on where you are in the buying cycle.

On LinkedIn, a lot of your potential clients are in the 'having a look' phase. So, they want to do their own 'window shopping'. And when you have a video they can watch passively, instead of having to get on a call with you to discuss the services you offer, they will jump on that opportunity.

What are some other equivalents on LinkedIn?

- You speaking to the person is your direct messaging once you are at the next level of buying interest.
- The eavesdropping is you reading the conversations in the comments on the speaker's article or post.
- The leaflet is your article or the blog on your website.
- The screen demo is your video.

Where to add video to your profile

As mentioned at the start of the chapter, it turns out you can add video or media files to many areas of your profile. The key ones to concentrate on, though, are your Featured section and your Experience section.

Your Featured section

This is the 'highlight reel' of your personal profile.

If you don't see a Featured section on your own profile, you might not have set this up yet.

How to create it:

- Go to your profile and click on 'Add profile section'.
- The Featured section appears in the 'Recommended' drop-down menu.

What kind of videos should you include here?

First, keep them short.

The ideal length for a video to add here is probably under a minute. People have short attention spans, and if you can't introduce yourself in less than one minute, they will already have moved on.

The role of this video can change over time. For example, I have linked to a short video from my recent speaking experience at UpLift Live on my profile. The core reason for this is that I am currently having conversations with at least two conference organisers, and they have both asked for video of me speaking at previous events.

You could add in an introductory video here. Speak into the camera and say hello to the people who are visiting your profile.

Here are a couple of examples:

- **Gillian Whitney** (www.linkedin.com/in/gillianwhitney), a live-stream strategist and coach, has links to video content on how to feel comfortable on camera in her Featured section.

- **Ciaran Armstrong** (www.linkedin.com/in/ciaran-armstrong) is doing a series of runs for Climate Action. He uses his Featured section to highlight his passion for his cause and pins posts rather than creating a separate video link. You can see the impact and message coming across clearly in his video.

How to add video to this section

You either need to link to a website that stores your video, such as Vimeo or YouTube, or you can upload a video post to LinkedIn and 'pin' it to your Featured section.

Both work well. However, it is my opinion that the link out to another site creates a slightly cleaner look and feel.

Your Experience section

Adding video to other sections boosts your profile. But, depending on the different sections of your profile where you are adding it, you want to be sure to share links to relevant video content.

For example, if your Experience section includes 'podcast host' and you have a link to a podcast video, add this to your Experience. Not only does this add extra weight to your profile, but the formatting is excellent. Great job, LinkedIn!

Where else?

You can also add video to the Honors & Awards, Volunteering and Education sections.

For the Education section, I think it would be powerful if you can upload video content from your final portfolio, or if you have a speech you have given relating to your qualification, or a demo of a tool you created, add it in!

Adding media to your Education section

You can add media to your existing Education by clicking on the little pencil icon in your Education section, scrolling to the bottom of the pop-up box and clicking on 'Add media'.

To include video, you must have an external link to add here – you cannot upload video to your profile directly.

Chapter **14**

Your LinkedIn Company Page

In this chapter:

This week I took two of my team out for lunch in Belfast. (If you are ever visiting Belfast, delicious gyozas can be found in the Dumpling Library!)

We always forget to take a photo if we are meeting in person. I guess if we specialised in Instagram, that might be first on the agenda. Lunch happened. Just no photos.

I was speaking to someone on the phone this week who is interested in working with us. He asked me a curious question.

He said, 'Who are those people on your website? Are they just some friends you got to come and join you in a photo shoot?'

They are my team.

It alerted me that maybe others don't realise we are a whole team.

These are some of the people in our team: we are currently seven – account manager, two writers, one operations manager, one graphic designer, one video editor and me. We also outsource podcast editing.

It takes a village.

You may not have a team yet, but unless you are just starting out I would think you are probably outsourcing some help. Hiring a virtual assistant? Work with someone to create your PowerPoint slides, like Fiona Walsh (www.linkedin.com/in/fionawalsh1), or talk to someone like Louise Ladd (www.linkedin.com/in/louiseladd), who can design beautiful documents and PDFs for you.

Top Tip

If you are starting out, as soon as you can afford to get help, do it!

You should be spending your time delivering the products and services you are an expert in. Not fiddling around with Canva and trying to slot in diary appointments. A professional support can do that stuff in 10% of the time it takes you. With a lot less frustration.

Are you sharing team photos and including your team in your LinkedIn marketing plans?

Don't worry, you don't need to be sharing photos of them (although this does of course help now and again), but I want to share some ways you can include your team and get them on board with the company LinkedIn marketing message.

First, let's look at the two different mediums on LinkedIn: the Company Page and the personal profile.

Company Pages and personal profiles

A lot of the content I post on LinkedIn is my personal profile content. However, we back it up with our Company Page, Louise Brogan Ltd – LinkedIn Content Marketing & Training (www.linkedin.com/company/linkinwithlouise).

I have always advocated for using a Company Page. Even when it was just me and one VA (virtual assistant) I had a Company Page.

The key reasons to have a Company Page are to:

- **market your business**
- **highlight your team**
- **attract and retain talent, and**
- **direct people to your company.**

The same reasons you might invest in sponsoring an industry event!

People are looking for your business and having a Company Page helps with SEO – the more ways someone can find your business, the better.

As we saw in Chapter 11, the Company Page is like the back-up band to your rock-star personal profile. Indulge me for a second while I revisit my Bruce Springsteen analogy …

When you think of Bruce Springsteen, what image springs to mind? One man on stage, or a band of 10 people with a frontman singing?

When you include your team in all your LinkedIn efforts, you multiply everything you do.

There is the rock star, Bruce. Then there is the whole machine behind him – the social media team, the management team, the record label, the merchandise branding and, of course, the whole of the E Street Band.

You are the rock star in this picture.

Your band are the Company Page. But, more than that, they are also engaging as individuals on the platform. Once you invest in training for your team, and they are comfortable posting and connecting with people, the next step is to help them amplify your company and business brand on LinkedIn. Let's look at a few ways to do this.

How to build your business brand with your team

Have a Company Page

A full tutorial on creating your Company Page[19] is available on our YouTube channel[20] and will walk you through exactly how to create one.

Do this even if you are a solo entrepreneur. Having a Company Page, fully optimised, helps your business to get found by search engines.

Include the Company Page on employee profiles

Encourage your team to include the Company Page on their LinkedIn personal profile by adding the correct link to their Experience section.

For your team members to add this, share the following steps:

- **click on the little + sign**
- **add the job title**
- **click on the drop-down menu and start typing your business name until the correct one appears**
- **select it.**

Now the company logo will appear on the employee's personal profile. This shows up not only in their Experience section, but also at the top on their Introductory Card.

Get your team on board

Bruce has the E Street Band appearing in his Instagram videos. They don't need to. I'm sure it is not part of their contract. But they can see that the more this happens, the more the brand grows.

[19] *See: https://youtube.com/playlist?list=PLEZMvQ5LF8O41deSM58fcuG_BQirBIi-2*
[20] *See: https://youtube.com/@raiseyourvisibilityonline*

It is in their best interest to get involved. It doesn't hurt if you have a great business to work for and your team want to support it.

This week I recorded some video of employees for a brand we have been working with for nine months. The most interesting part for me was finding out how much these team members enjoyed working for this client.

It might take a little time to persuade your team to get involved in the content creation process for the business, but if you can, do it!

Incentivise your team

You could incentivise them through rewards, or simply by explaining the reason behind your request.

Our team know why we do what we do. They are on board with the mission we have: to raise the visibility of our clients on LinkedIn.

The incentive for them?

To grow the business, have a stable job, have input into how we work with clients, and the occasional dumpling-filled lunch.

Are your team helping you to build the brand on LinkedIn?

I see a couple of different scenarios:

No one is allowed to use LinkedIn for fear of recruiters swiping your best talent. If your company focuses on being the best place to work, why would they leave you?

But also – people move on, move up, and have goals and ambitions of their own. Why not make your company appealing to the best talent out there?

Company Pages are not just there to market products and services. They are also a way to attract and retain the best talent.

Maybe your boss dictates from above that the team need to use LinkedIn but hasn't given you any ideas on how to do this. If so, ask for some proper training on what to do.

LinkedIn training for companies

I have found that larger organisations benefit from two-tier training.

The marketing team have a workshop on the best set-up, the content that works, the strategy needed for LinkedIn.

Then the team have training on their own profiles, and how to use what the marketing team have created, to build not only the business but their own professional network.

We offer corporate workshops and strategies to help you amplify your business on LinkedIn, in a non-sleazy, people-oriented way.

If you want to recruit new staff, they will be checking out your business online and the Company Page can showcase it as a potential place of work.

As your company grows, your team can share your business story with their audience, and can also contribute to creating content on the Company Page.

Think of this as amplifying your team members. Someone from your company appears on a stage, speaks on a podcast or is interviewed in the media. Having your business branding behind them gives more weight to their presence, both on- and offline.

Why a LinkedIn Company Page is the main hub for your business

The Company Page is where you can tell your company story, posting news and updates, and sending out marketing-related content.

Many of you, of course, may be working as a solopreneur or with a very small team. Even so, when you have a Company Page, you can add your own logo and company details to your personal profile.

Filling in the About summary and tag line of the Company Page using the keywords that your ideal client is searching for gives you more chances of being found by that client. Why would you not want that extra visibility?

One of our clients, Scientific Writers, has really embraced its LinkedIn Company Page and posts weekly newsletters aimed at its ideal audience. Its CEO, Dr Allison Kirsop, comments:

Since maximising our Company Page by adding to the Featured section and starting a regular newsletter, we've seen an increase in engagement from our network and identified potential new clients. I'm convinced of two things: by showcasing our team and with employee buy-in to our marketing efforts, we are raising awareness of who we are and what we do. It's a long game, but following up on engagement has also given us new contacts and areas to explore.

Measure what works

How many people follow your page? How many new followers have you gained? How many people are being presented with your posts?

You can find this information by clicking on the Analytics tab of your page admin view. Only someone who works as a page admin has access to the analytics.

Keep a record of how your page is performing, and if the numbers start to increase in line with more engagement on your posts, you know you are on the right track.

For some organisations, clients will reach out to find out about your products and services without ever commenting on your page posts.

This is a very common scenario on LinkedIn.

Your job is to make sure that, if someone is looking for your products/services, your Company Page reflects that and leads to enquiries. One good indicator is an increase in the number of 'custom button clicks'.

What's the difference between impressions and views?

Impressions are the number of times your post appears in the newsfeed of someone on the LinkedIn platform. This does not mean that they have interacted or engaged with your post, simply that it has been served up to them on-screen.

Check your visitor demographics

Under the Analytics drop-down menu, click on 'Visitors' and have a look at who is following your page. Do they fit your ideal client profile?

Who is visiting your sponsor booth or picking up your freebies at the next event you attend? Are you following up those leads?

Leverage your employees

One of your best strategies for promoting your organisation on LinkedIn is to leverage your employees. Invite your team to link to the Company Page on the Experience section of their personal profiles.

Create a strategy for your company to encourage your team members to share the Company Page content to their own personal networks.

In the next chapter, you'll find more information about how to include your employees.

Improve internal communications via the My Company tab

The purpose of the My Company tab is to allow companies to create an employees-only space on their LinkedIn page. This feature is initially available only to pages with more than 200 employees registered on LinkedIn, and only employees of the company will be able to see this tab and its content … However, see the top tip!

Top Tip I have a client with fewer than 200 employees who has access to this, so check your own page. You might be surprised!

One of the aims of having a 'trusted' space on LinkedIn inside a Company Page is to encourage employees to connect while working remotely. It's a space where they can collectively celebrate wins and milestones, and get to know one another a little better.

Another aim is to give companies an easy way to keep their colleagues informed of the latest news within the company.

To access this feature, go to your LinkedIn page and click on the My Company tab in the left-hand menu. All organisations that qualify for the My Company tab will have it added automatically.

Now, I love the idea of this feature. The reality, though, is that you need to deploy a little extra help. Most employees don't tend to dander[21] over to the My Company tab.

Setting up a system whereby your team get a reminder to check the My Company tab will give this the extra little boost you need.

Connecting your employees to the Company Page

Employees must self-identify as working for your company, so invite them to connect to your page. They can add your company under the Experience section of their personal profile; take a look at my article here to find out more: 'How to write a great LinkedIn profile'.[22]

When someone adds your company to the Experience section of their profile, they'll be added to your company's employees. If you discover someone on the My Company tab who isn't an employee, your page admin can contact LinkedIn support to report inaccurate employment.[23]

Content on the My Company tab

Each employee's experience on the My Company tab will differ depending on who they're connected to and where they're located. For example, you could have a group of colleagues all based in California, or a group of software engineers.

The top section highlights company news, the stock price (if relevant), and new employees or co-workers. If employees click on a new co-worker's name, they can send a connection request directly from the My Company tab.

The next section, Trending Co-worker Content, displays posts from co-workers, encouraging staff to interact with one another via their posts. This will also help employees find co-workers with common interests.

The content shared in this section will be determined by the LinkedIn algorithm. According to LinkedIn, employees are 60% more likely to engage with posts from their co-workers than other connections, and 14 times more likely to share content from their Company Page.

---

[21] *'What's the Craic? NI Vocab Guide', Queen's University Belfast, 13 March 2023. Available at: https://qub.ac.uk/student-blog/belfast-ni/new-ni-vocab.html*

[22] *See: https://louisebrogan.com/how-to-write-a-great-linkedin-profile/*

[23] *'Remove people from a LinkedIn Page', https://linkedin.com/help/linkedin/answer/1589*

All LinkedIn Company Pages with more than 200 employees registered on LinkedIn will automatically have the Trending Co-worker Content feature turned on. Only a LinkedIn page admin can turn this feature on or off.

Finally, the Grow Your Network section will display a list of suggested connections within the company. The connections are based on location, which team the employee works with, and mutual co-worker connections.

With more employees working from home for the foreseeable future, LinkedIn is helping companies connect with and support their employees with three new features for Company Pages: the My Company tab, Events tab, and Followers Analytics.

While there has been a tendency to focus on personal profiles on LinkedIn, these features will help businesses encourage their employees to interact with their Company Page, as well as reach new audiences.

Company Page case study

LinkedIn pages can also produce articles and newsletters.

The following case study is from Sarah Reveillard, former global social and content lead for Microsoft Advertising. A key part of Sarah's role at Microsoft was to enable the growth of the Microsoft Advertising LinkedIn Company Page in terms of engagement and followership (53k+ followers).

The case study presents some key learnings Sarah and her team were able to take away from experimenting extensively with LinkedIn page articles.

Case Study The power of storytelling with LinkedIn articles for pages

Sarah Reveillard, former global social and content lead, Microsoft Advertising

Microsoft Advertising published more than 10 LinkedIn articles in 2021 and the results were fantastic in the following three ways.

Great for search engine ranking and great for the customer

One of our LinkedIn articles features the transcript of Microsoft Advertising podcast, *The Download*,[24] and one of the many benefits is that the podcast episode can be embedded into the article for a better customer experience (see below). It is also possible to embed YouTube videos.

This is a great way to cross-promote the channels too. For example, adding the LinkedIn article transcript link to Spotify and YouTube is a great way to bring new visitors, and potentially followers, to our LinkedIn channel.

Another key benefit is that LinkedIn articles are indexed on search engine results, so this is a great way to rank well from a search engine optimisation (SEO) point of view. Articles for pages also give access to detailed audience insights, including 'the firmographics of people reading and interacting with the content'.

Great for events in your own industry

One of the most successful uses of LinkedIn articles has been the recap summary of a retail webinar series encapsulating different markets and user cases. To extend the longevity of the article, each customer success story was posted organically on Microsoft Advertising social channels at one-week intervals, which meant this one article drove three times more views than average, and a great deal of shares and engagements. That tactic has been quite powerful post-event.

Additionally, a key benefit from LinkedIn Company Page organic is that it's possible to target by language and other firmographics (see below). It means that for global organisations such as Microsoft Advertising, this feature has been a powerful way to create and publish bespoke social posts in different languages, while tagging the customer and colleagues involved to strengthen our customer relationships.

Great for humanising brands

Another very successful way we've been using LinkedIn articles is for an initiative in Australia where our colleagues at Microsoft Advertising have been closely involved in support of mental health. An increasing trend in content marketing is for brands to not just talk about themselves but also shine a light on their employees by featuring their work. Using LinkedIn articles is a great way to give our brand and our colleagues a voice for such an important topic, especially during these strange times. This article has helped us to deepen our community engagement at a time where empathy and connectivity are more important than ever.

To conclude, I will say that the launch of LinkedIn articles has been a fantastic way for Microsoft Advertising to connect more closely with everyone: customers, peers and people. Thought leadership can take many forms, from industry insight to purpose-driven vision to transparent introspection and beyond. With articles for pages, brands have that flexibility.

[24] *'Taylor Lorenz on internet culture and its influence on ads', Microsoft Advertising, 9 November 2021, https://linkedin.com/pulse/taylor-lorenz-internet-culture-its-influence-ads-/*

Chapter **15**

How to include your employees

In this chapter:

LinkedIn Events

LinkedIn Events[25] was relaunched in early 2020 for both personal profiles and Company Pages. To make events easier to find and encourage more interaction with employees and followers, events are now available in the left-hand menu of Company Pages.

Events are listed in chronological order on the Events tab and only page admins can cancel events or delete them from the page.

When LinkedIn members click on this tab, they can see all your page's upcoming events. From here, they sign up for an event or share it with their network.

When people sign up for your event, that event will appear in their personal profile alongside any previous events they've hosted or attended. This information is visible only to that person.

Collect and download registrant information for LinkedIn Events

If you are going to the effort to create an event on your LinkedIn profile, I suggest you use your page for this.

When your event is posted on the page, you get to collect registration details.

Remember we are in business. Getting registered attendees means data – who is interested in your webinar? I bet they must have an interest in what your business offers too.

This is why page events are so good.

LinkedIn uses registration forms for pages that organise events. When someone signs up for your event, they complete a simple registration form, pulling information from their profile.

This functionality will be available for public events only. Adding the registration form to your event will make it mandatory for people to complete the form to attend the event.

Note that, to use this tool, you must have a privacy policy on your company website.

Following the event, event organisers can download the registration information from the Manage Attendees section of the event. LinkedIn members who attend

[25] *See: https://louisebrogan.com/linkedin-events/*

your event can choose to opt out of consent to be contacted further by you following the event.

Everyone is happy!

Plus, if you are staying inside the internet, 'best practice rules'. Any email you send to someone who has opted in to your email list will have an 'Unsubscribe' button at the bottom, so they can choose if they still want to hear from you or not.

Please don't scrape email addresses and send out cold-calling emails to ideal clients without permission.

Yes, if you throw enough spaghetti at the wall, some of it will stick. But we are inviting our pasta lovers in with the aroma of our sauce, not flinging it at them from the window.

Live streaming on Company Pages

LinkedIn is encouraging Company Pages to use LinkedIn Live to host virtual events. Once an event has finished, the live stream will be available on the Company Page as a video.

One of our clients is running regular free webinars with its ops manager and design team to show the inner workings of how they create programmes for their clients.

They also like to host events discussing the trends in the industry.

How to be seen as a thought leader in your space – take the microphone and take the stage, my friend. The first time is always the scariest.

Once I did a whole webinar and forgot to hit record so couldn't send out the promised replay. Another time on a Live Event, the guest forgot to turn up and I had to create the training out of thin air. Well not quite. Luckily for me, I can talk about my business easily, but I usually prefer this to happen with planning rather than due to circumstance.

Types of content to share on your Company Page

- If you are creating regular content for your business, this is where you can share it on LinkedIn. For example, if you create a weekly blog or podcast, share this on your Company Page.

- Share a regular video from yourself or your team. A quick way for your viewers to engage with your company is to connect via video; see my article 'How to use LinkedIn Live and LinkedIn Video for your business'[26] for further info. For example, you could share a 'vox pop'-style video where a member of staff discusses their thoughts on a particular topic.
- Share updates from your company – events you are hosting or attending, either online or in person. Creating your events on LinkedIn allows you to invite your followers and drum up interest.
- Use your page to highlight business partners and relationships – a win-win for everyone involved.

Why a Company Page is good for your team

If you have a team working with you in your business, then having a Company Page is an excellent idea for LinkedIn. Here's why:

- You can highlight your team and their achievements.
- Your team can add your business to their personal profile Experience section, giving them more credibility.

I suggest you include your employees in creating the Company Page strategy if you can. Rather than dictate to them, bring them along with you.

How to include your employees in the LinkedIn company strategy

Provide your employees with some basic training on how to use LinkedIn.

We provide different levels of training for our clients' employees – from short 45-minute workshops on why the company is using LinkedIn, to wider profile training and content creation. Investing in your team benefits everyone.

Encourage your employees to share company-created content. When you have a team who are creating relevant, branded and interesting content, invite your employees to share that content with your network.

[26] *See: https://louisebrogan.com/how-to-use-linkedin-live-and-linkedin-video-for-your-business/*

Use LinkedIn employee advocacy tools

There are several ways to engage your employees on your LinkedIn Company Page. LinkedIn makes this easy for you, as page admin, to do.

- You can use the 'Notify Employees' tool: when you post on your Company Page, you can click on the three little dots at the top right of the post and a drop-down menu will appear, with the option to 'Notify Employees'. This tool is available to use once every 24 hours and you can notify every employee who is attached to the Company Page. Then they can like the post, comment on it and/or share it.
- Empower your team by showing them how to effectively share content from the Company Page.
- Highlight your team in your posts. When an employee becomes the feature of the post, they will be more inclined to share it with their network.

Top Tip Teach your employees to include their own thoughts on the topic when sharing content. Simply sharing a post to their own newsfeed without commentary will have less impact.

Share your employees' content on the Company Page

LinkedIn will showcase your employees' content in the Admin view of your page. This will be easier to use when you are a larger organisation and have more active employees on LinkedIn.

Leverage your senior executives

LinkedIn data show that employees typically have 10 times the engagement on their personal posts and with their own network vs Company Page posts. Ask your executive team to mention the Company Page in their posts, using the @ mention.

Reward employees who engage with your activities

Incentivise your team to get involved in your company's marketing efforts on LinkedIn.

Why not host a quarterly 'prize' event, highlighting those who are helping the business grow on LinkedIn. The prize could be related to helping their social media efforts, or could simply be a feature on the page.

LinkedIn recommends that organisations outsource content creation and scheduling to external agencies – for example, to carry out the following tasks.

- Respond to comments and questions from page followers. Have a team and process in place. You can now reply on the mobile app.
- Consider an agency for your scheduling and community management, so you can focus more on strategy.

Here at LinkedIn with Louise, we offer both strategy and management.

Just as the speaker on the stage doesn't know everyone in their audience, you will not know everyone in your LinkedIn network.

And like your audience at a conference, only a handful of people will come up to you and introduce themselves.

The key is to keep showing up and reminding people who you are and what you do.

Build your audience steadily. Keep getting on the stage and keep your message coming out to people.

When was the last time you reached out to someone you admire on LinkedIn with a message? You might be surprised at the results.

In preparation for this book, I messaged a lot of people who are in my network. From nuclear engineers and career coaches to the head of advertising at Microsoft and PowerPoint specialists, pharmaceutical consultants and the head of data at BT Group.

All of these people are normal, like you and me. They embrace the opportunities given by using their platform on LinkedIn. Few of the contributors have large networks beyond 10,000 people.

The common thread is that they connect, have conversations and are using LinkedIn as a tool to help drive their business and career forward. All without spamming their network.

In conclusion

LinkedIn provides the opportunity to raise your profile online in front of the people you want to work with. Spend time optimising your profile. Decide what content you want to share with your audience. Connect thoughtfully with people. Build a network of value, full of people you find interesting and want to have conversations with. Imagine your LinkedIn represents your favourite industry conference and present yourself in the same way. Talk to people and enjoy it. You never know where it may lead!

This book is just the beginning.

We have lots of resources to help guide you on your way with LinkedIn – from a free library of videos, webinars and blogs to useful checklists and workbooks.

- Visit www.raiseyourvisibilityonline.com to access these resources, and much more.
- Connect with me on LinkedIn at www.linkedin.com/in/louisebrogan
- Subscribe to my YouTube channel at www.youtube.com/@raiseyourvisibilityonline

I'll be cheering you on every step of the way!

Printed in Great Britain
by Amazon

57893944R00086